The British Horse Society
STAGE 1
WORKBOOK

A study and revision aid for exam candidates

Melissa Troup BA, BHSII and
Margaret Linington-Payne MA (Ed), BHSI

KENILWORTH PRESS

First published in the UK in 2008 by Kenilworth Press, an imprint of
Quiller Publishing Ltd

Reprinted 2010

British Library Cataloguing in Publication Data
A catalogue record for this book is available from the British Library

ISBN 978-905693-22-1

Layout and illustrations by Carole Vincer
Cover design and prelims by Sharyn Troughton

Printed in Malta by Gutenberg Press Ltd

KENILWORTH PRESS
An imprint of Quiller Publishing Ltd
Wykey House, Wykey, Shrewsbury
Shropshire, SY4 1JA
tel: 01939 261616 fax: 01939 261606
e-mail: info@quillerbooks.com
website: www.kenilworthpress.com

CONTENTS

INTRODUCTION

This workbook has been compiled as a revision aid for candidates preparing for the BHS Stage 1 exam. It is designed to be used in conjunction with a Stage 1 course, ideally provided by a BHS Where to Train Centre, where instructors have a good understanding of the BHS examination system.

The questions have been written to captivate the imagination and help to make revision and quizzing of knowledge entertaining, whilst maintaining the integrity of the quality of the exam for which the student is preparing.

The authors wish to stress that there is no 'BHS way' for either practical or theory. As such there may be more answers to questions than have been given. The BHS system aims to train practical, safe and efficient horsemen and women, thus providing a foundation of internationally recognised qualifications from which a person may develop in any equestrian direction.

Details of further reading and contact details for the BHS are given at the end of the book.

1 GROOMING

Q1.1 Identify and describe the purpose of each of these grooming kit items.

A
B
C
D
E
F
G
H
I
J
K
L

A		
B		
C		
D		
E		
F		
G		
H		
I		
J		
K		
L		

Q1.2 Below is a list of reasons for grooming. Explain each.

Health

Condition

Prevention of disease

Appearance

Checking for new heat/swelling

Cleanliness

Q1.3 Put the grooming sequence in a correct order for brushing off. (1–4)

Brushing off

- [ ] • Sponge eyes, nose and dock
- [ ] • Pick out the feet
- [ ] • Brush the body
- [ ] • Tie up the horse

Q1.4 Put the grooming sequence in a correct order for quartering. (1–10)

Quartering

- [ ] • Undo and secure the rug fastenings
- [ ] • Tie up the horse
- [ ] • Fold the front of the rug back
- [ ] • Fold the rear of the rug forward
- [ ] • Sponge eyes, nose and dock
- [ ] • Pick out the feet
- [ ] • Brush the front of the body and mane
- [ ] • Clean the tail
- [ ] • Secure the rug
- [ ] • Brush the back of the horse

Q1.5 Grooming – can you spot eight unsafe practices in this picture? List them in the space below.

1._____

2._____

3 _____

4._____

5._____

6._____

7._____

8._____

Q1.6 Below is a sequence of images for putting on a tail bandage, but the order is jumbled. Match the sentences to the drawings to describe the correct sequence.

5 return back up the tail   6 tie tapes on the side

4 wrap evenly all the way down to the base of the tail   1 start the bandage with the end flap out

7 fold the last wrap over the bow   3 roll bandage over flap   2 fold flap over

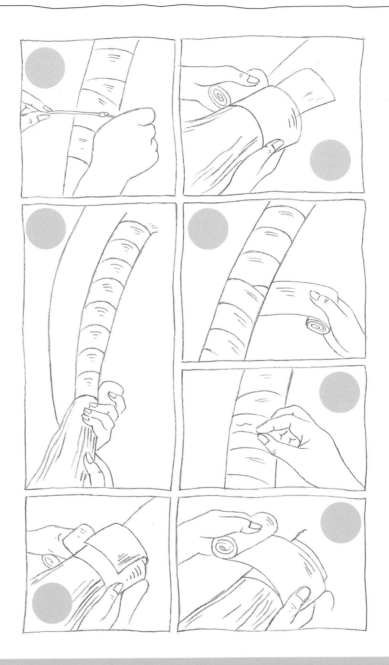

Q1.7 Fill in the missing words to describe how you would remove a tail bandage.

To remove a tail bandage, firstly _____ the tapes and possibly loosen the first few wraps of the

_____. Holding the top of the bandage, gently _____ it down the tail. Re-roll ready for use.

2 CLOTHING

Q2.1 Identify these rugs and state when they could be used.

_____

_____

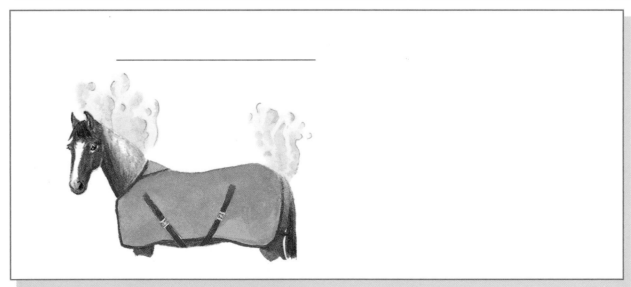

_____

Q2.2 Match the sentences to the cartoon strip to describe how to put on a rug.

1 Securely tie up the horse.
2 Place the rug over the horse's withers.
3 Fasten the front strap.
4 Unfold the rug.
5 Secure the surcingle straps, crossing them underneath the horse's stomach.
6 Fasten the leg straps/pull the tail over the fillet string.

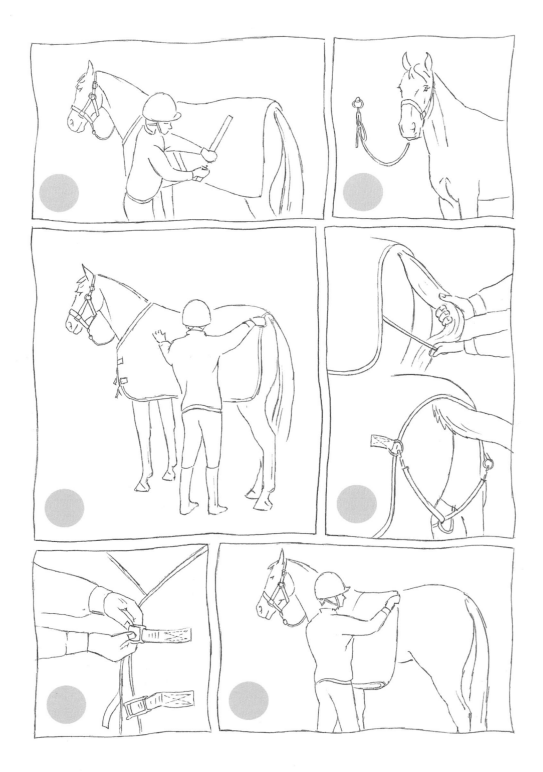

Q2.3 Label and describe the areas of good fit on the rug below.

Q2.4 Label and describe the areas of poor fit on the rug below.

Q2.5 Number these images in the correct sequence to show how to fasten leg straps. Two of the images are incorrect – can you spot them?

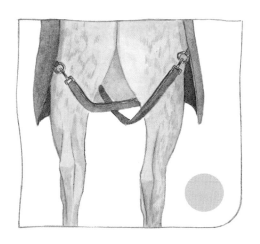

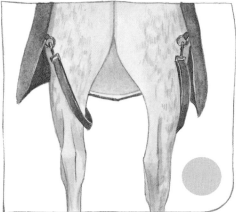

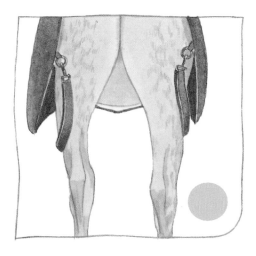

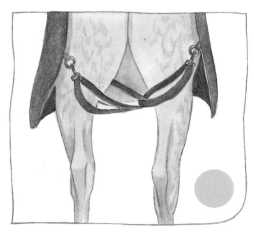

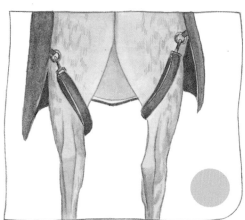

Q2.6 Consider whether the following statements describing a correct, safe method to remove a rug are true or false. Tick the appropriate boxes.

STATEMENT	True	False
The horse should be securely tied, using a headcollar and quick-release knot.		
The fastenings are undone from the front to the back.		
The fastenings are undone from the back to the front.		
The rug is folded front half over back half, and then slid back over the horse's hindquarters and removed.		
The fastenings are tied up before removal to prevent them injuring the horse.		

Q2.7 These jumbled descriptions refer to stable rugs, New Zealands and coolers. Can you work out which is which and write them in the chart below? (Some apply to more than one type of rug.)

Some have tail flaps   Durable   Non-waterproof

Duvet-like filling   Usually has leg straps

Maintains warmth whilst allowing the horse to cool down

Tough   Wicks away moisture from the horse

Usually has a fillet string   Waterproof

STABLE	NEW ZEALAND	COOLER

3 SADDLERY

Q3.1 Label as many parts of the saddle as you can.

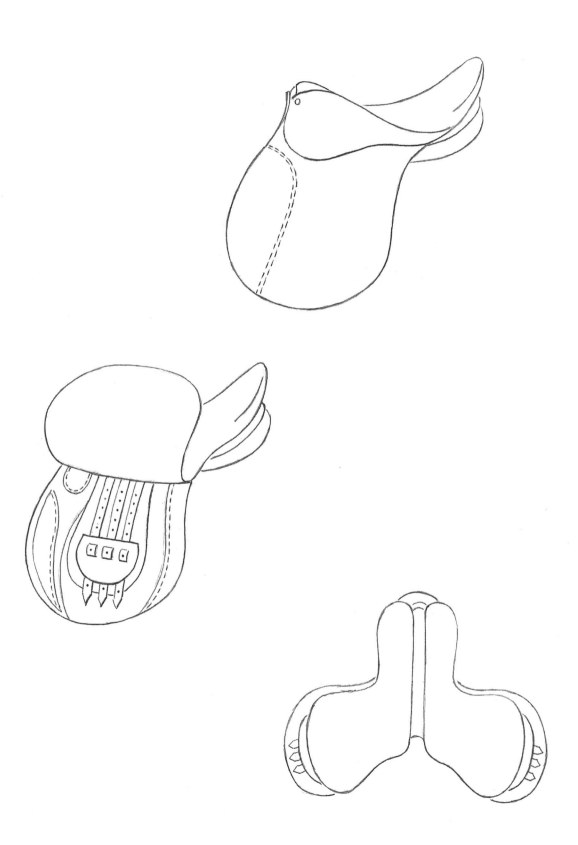

Q3.2 Label the parts of the bridle.

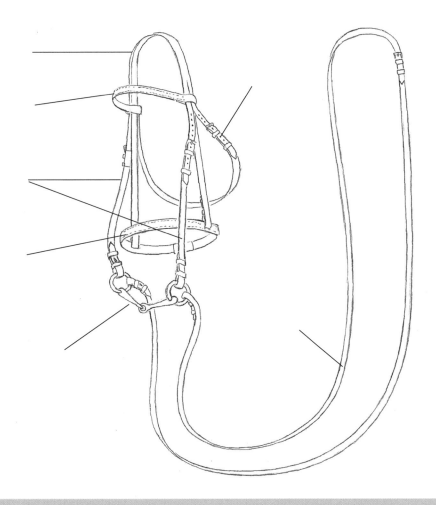

Q3.3 When putting on a saddle, what should you check to ensure the horse's comfort? List as many points as you can.

_____

_____

_____

_____

_____

_____

_____

Q3.4 Look at these drawings of a running and a standing martingale. Describe points to remember for the comfort of the horse.

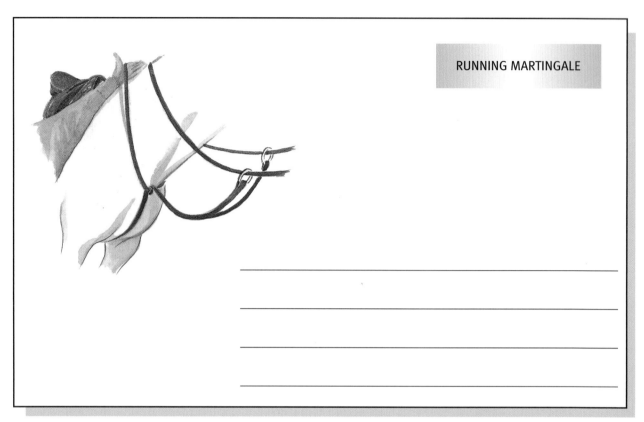

RUNNING MARTINGALE

_____

_____

_____

_____

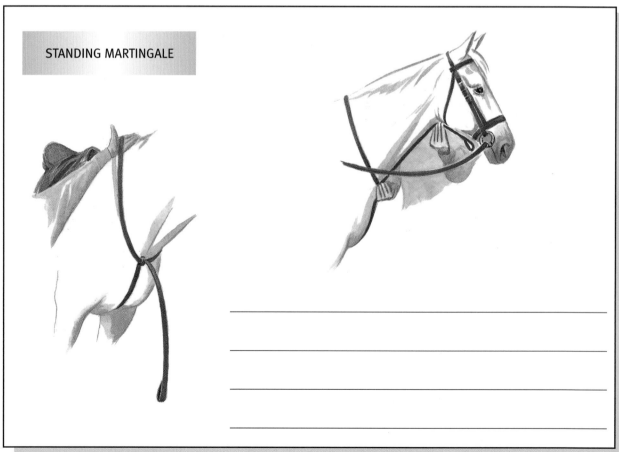

STANDING MARTINGALE

_____

_____

_____

Q3.5 Describe how you would put on a hunting breastplate.

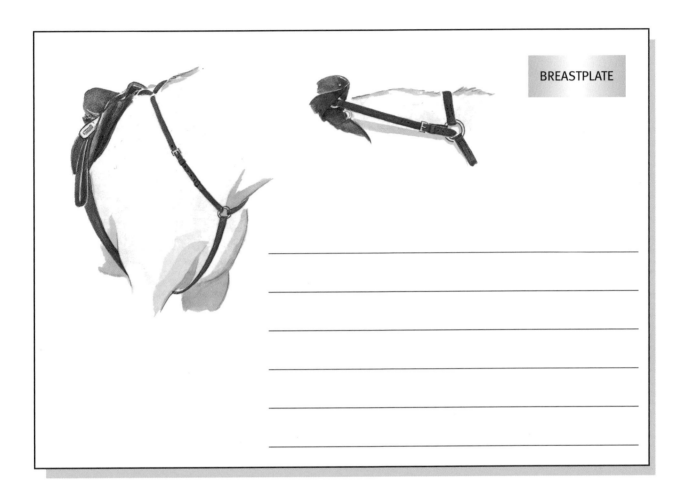

BREASTPLATE

_____

_____

_____

_____

_____

_____

Q3.6 Finish the table listing the consequences of dirty or worn tack.

DIRTY GIRTH	
THIN STIRRUP LEATHERS	
WORN STITCHING ON STIRRUP LEATHERS	
DIRTY NUMNAH	
WORN STITCHES ON GIRTH STRAPS	

Q3.7 Tacking up. Number the pictures from 1–10, putting them into sequence and describe the correct tacking-up procedure at each stage.

1 _____

2 _____

3 _____

4 _____

5 _____

6 _____

7 _____

8 _____

9 _____

10 _____

Shipley College

Q3.8 Untacking. Number the pictures from 1–10, putting them into sequence, and describe the correct untacking procedure at each stage.

1 _____

2 _____

3 _____

4 _____

5 _____

6 _____

7 _____

8 _____

9 _____

10 _____

Q3.9 (a) In what sizes are numnahs produced?
(b) Fill in the gaps, using the words provided, to describe how to fit a numnah.

(a) _____

forward	gullet	loops	numnah	saddle	hair

(b) Place the _____ on the horse's back a little further _____ than the position of the

the saddle. Place the _____ on top and pull the numnah up into the _____ of the

saddle. Slide both saddle and numnah back into the correct position; this aids the _____ to lie

flat. Attach the numnah to the saddle by the _____ usually positioned for the girth.

Q3.10 Name the types of noseband shown below and opposite. Describe their action and
fastening.

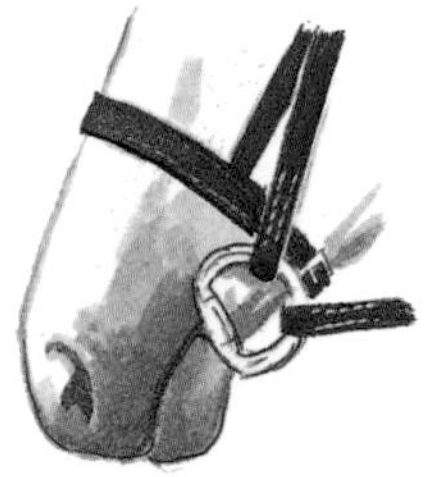

Q3.11 (a) Explain the purpose of each stage of tack cleaning.
(b) What is the reason for 'stripping' tack?

(a)_____

_____

_____

_____

(b)_____

_____

_____

_____

4 HANDLING

Q4.1 Below is a yard scene filled with hazards. Circle the areas of potential danger to horse and people.

Q4.2 Explain the following principles of handling and working with horses.

SAFETY

RISK ASSESSMENTS

RESPECT BETWEEN HORSE AND GROOM

COMMUNICATION

DISCIPLINE

ROUTINE

Q4.3 Using the words provided, fill in the gaps to explain how to put on and fit a headcollar.

shoulder	poll	lead rope	two fingers'	head	noseband

Prepare the headcollar ready to use by unravelling the _____ if rolled, ensuring that the

_____ is done up and that the headpiece is undone. Approach the horse at his _____.

Standing just in front of the shoulder, facing the horse's _____, lift the noseband over the nose.

Position the headpiece over the _____, avoiding the ears and fasten the buckle. To check the

fit, the noseband should have_____ width below the projecting cheek bone and two

fingers' width between the noseband and the face.

Q4.4 (a) List three basic safety checks that you might make before being happy to tie up a horse in an unknown environment.
(b) Number these images of tying a quick-release knot in the correct sequence.

(a) _____

_____

(b)

Q4.5 Why is it important to use time efficiently, as well as being safe, when working with horses?

_____

_____

_____

_____

5 HORSE HUSBANDRY

Q5.1 Fill in the gaps in the table with appropriate comments on the various types of bedding.

BEDDING	STRAW	SHAVINGS	HEMP	PAPER	RUBBER MATTING
EXPENSIVE	Depends on season				Initial cost
EDIBLE					No
EASY STORAGE				Yes	
EASY DISPOSAL			Yes		
DUSTY					No
COMFORT					
CLEAN					Always use with bedding

Q5.2 List four reasons why we use bedding.

1. _____

2. _____

3. _____

4. _____

Q5.3 Fill in the gaps to make sense of the paragraph describing mucking out.

mucked out	draughts	bedding	thinner	lie down	bedding	skipped out

Although types of _____ vary, maintenance is fairly similar. They are generally _____ once per day and _____ every time you enter the stable. Day beds tend to be _____ , with the bedding thrown up into the banks. More _____ may be added to night beds so that the horse has a thicker bed in which to _____ at night. Banks are built to preclude _____ and to prevent the horse from becoming cast.

Q5.4 List the advantages and disadvantages of daily mucking out and deep littering.

ADVANTAGES	DISADVANTAGES

DAILY MUCKING OUT

DEEP LITTERING

Q5.5 Mucking out. Put the list below into the correct order from 1–8 to explain the correct procedure.

- [ ] • Lay the bed.
- [ ] • Remove the water buckets.
- [ ] • Throw all the bedding up onto one bank (rotated daily).
- [ ] • Remove the horse from the stable or tie up securely.
- [ ] • Sweep the floor.
- [ ] • Remove the wet area.
- [ ] • Replace the freshly filled water buckets.
- [ ] • Remove the droppings.

Q5.6 Explain the terms 'skipping out' and 'setting fair'.

_____

_____

_____

_____

Q5.7 Describe how to maintain a muck heap that has three separate heaps.

_____

_____

_____

_____

_____

_____

Q5.8 Below is a picture of a stable being incorrectly mucked out. List the four mistakes being made.

1._____

2._____

3._____

4._____

6 THE FOOT AND SHOEING

Q6.1 Picking out the feet. Describe what is happening in each picture.

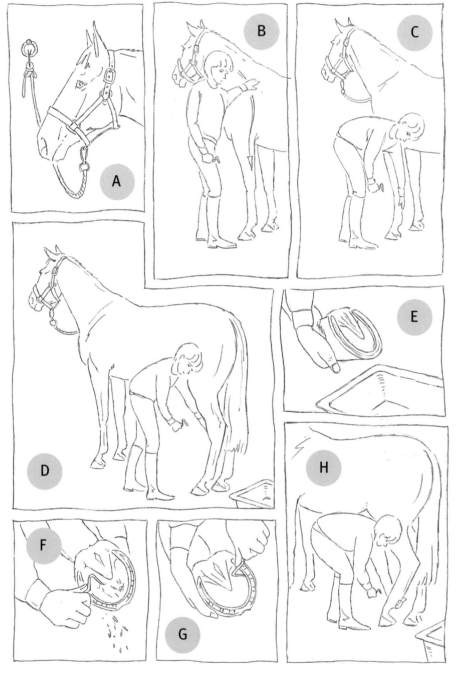

A _____

B _____

C _____

D _____

E _____

F _____

G _____

H _____

Q6.2 Fill in the gaps, using the words provided, to explain how to wash and oil the horse's feet.

| light   water   hooves   scrub |

Using a _____ brush, clean the outside of the _____. Pick up each foot in turn and

gently _____ the underside of each hoof. Once the feet are dry, oil inside and out using a

_____ oil.

Q6.3 Match these shoeing terms to their correct definitions.

Term
Recently shod
In need of shoeing
Risen clenches
Sprung shoe
Loose shoe
Cast shoe
Worn thin
Long feet
Overgrown foot

Meaning	Term
thin, wafer-like shoes that may actually snap	
the shoe has come off	
shod one or two weeks ago	
as the toe grows, it takes the shoe forward causing the clenches to rise	
the shoe is not flat on the horse's foot; it may be pulled away from the foot and be bent	
many horses grow more at the toe than at the heel and therefore give the impression of long toes	
growth over the sides of the shoe	
the foot requires attention	
movement of the shoe when examined	

Q6.4 Label these diagrams to show the key points of a well-shod foot.

Q6.5 This foot (below and opposite top) is in need of shoeing. Can you label the tell-tale signs?

Q6.6 Label as many external parts of the foot as you can.

Q6.7 What could be the consequences of irregular shoeing?

7 ANATOMY AND HANDLING

Q7.1 Label the points of a horse.

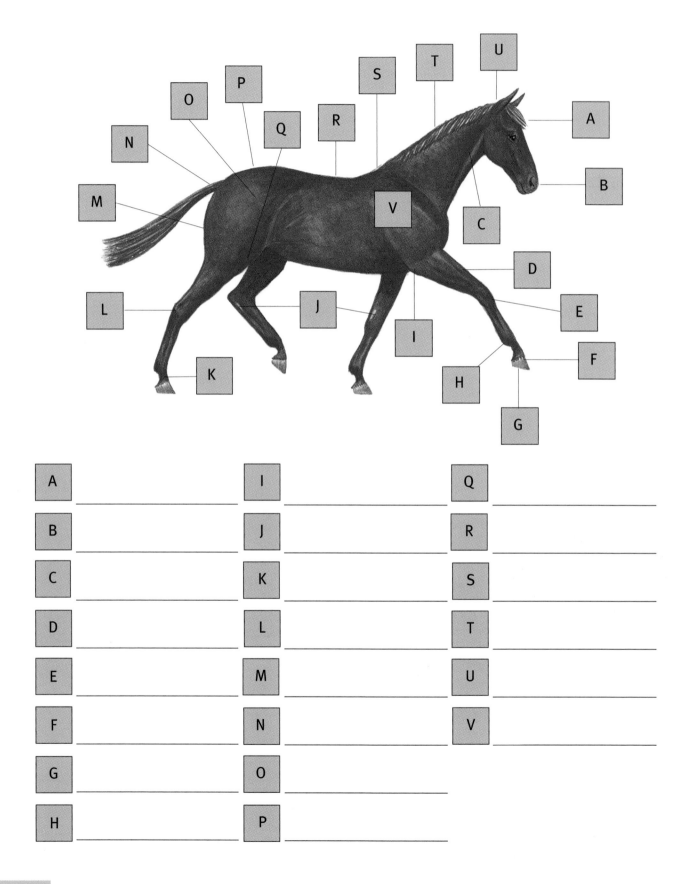

A	_____	I	_____	Q	_____
B	_____	J	_____	R	_____
C	_____	K	_____	S	_____
D	_____	L	_____	T	_____
E	_____	M	_____	U	_____
F	_____	N	_____	V	_____
G	_____	O	_____		
H	_____	P	_____		

Q7.2 Describe each of these horse colours.

BAY	
GREY	
CHESTNUT	
BLACK	
BROWN	
DUN	
PALOMINO	
PIEBALD	
SKEWBALD	
SPOTTED	
ROAN	

Q7.3 There are further terms to describe greys and spotted horses. Label each picture.

GREY

_____

_____

_____

SPOTTED

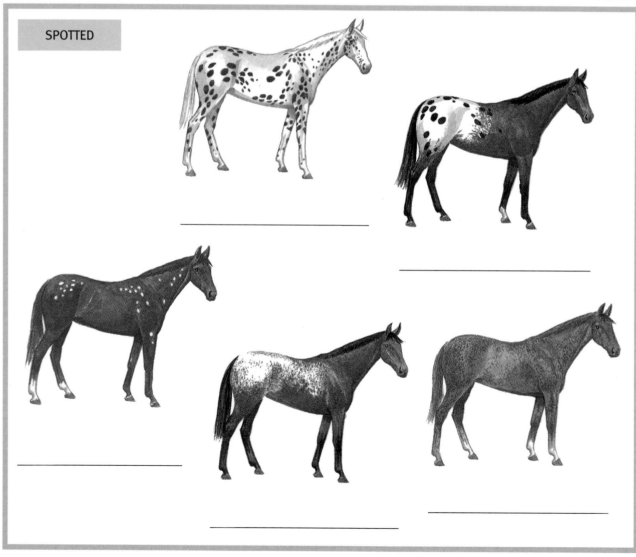

_____

_____

_____

_____

_____

Q7.4 Name each of these facial markings.

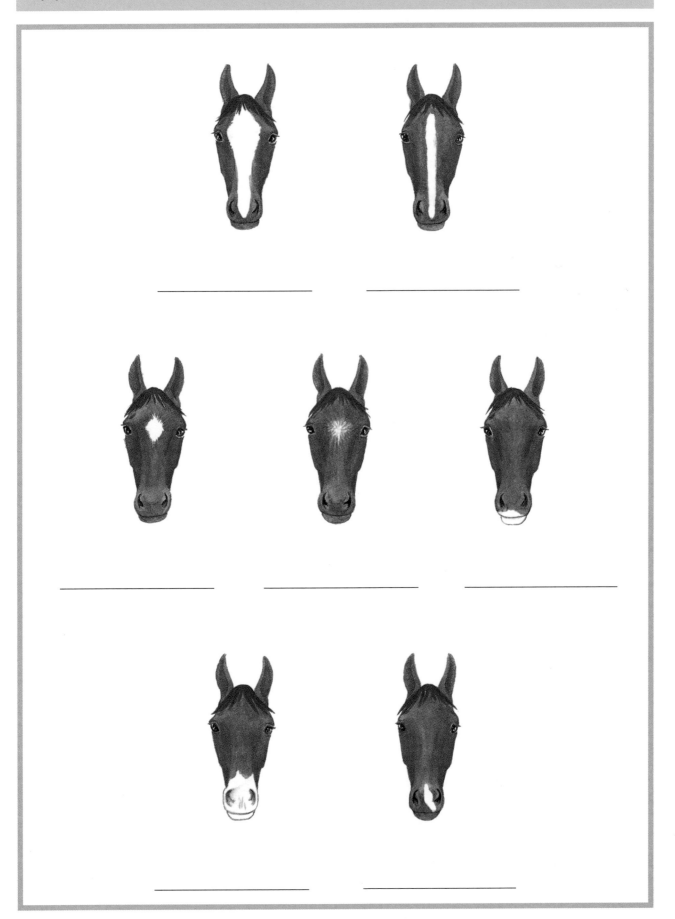

Q7.5 Colour in each blank leg to show the markings named below.

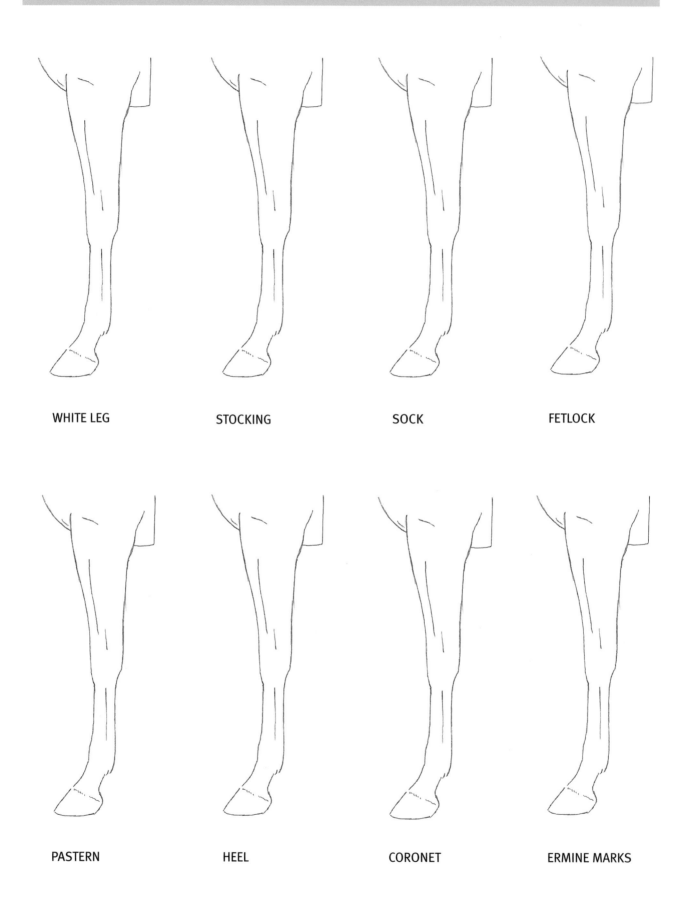

WHITE LEG   STOCKING   SOCK   FETLOCK

PASTERN   HEEL   CORONET   ERMINE MARKS

Q7.6 Describe each of these markings.

MEALY MUZZLE	
TOAD EYE	
DORSAL LINE	
ZEBRA MARKINGS	
WHORL	
INJURY MARKING	

Q7.7 List the differences and the similarities between holding a horse for treatment and standing for inspection?

DIFFERENCES

SIMILARITIES

Q7.8 Write a checklist of all that you like about the way this unknown horse is being led in walk.

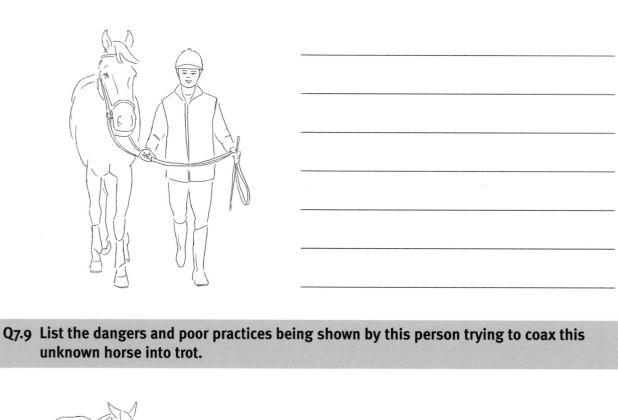

_____

_____

_____

_____

_____

_____

Q7.9 List the dangers and poor practices being shown by this person trying to coax this unknown horse into trot.

_____

_____

_____

_____

_____

Q7.10 Describe the correct way to turn a horse when led in hand.

_____

_____

_____

8 HEALTH AND SAFETY

Q8.1 List five stable-yard situations where regular lifting could be hazardous.

1._____

2._____

3._____

4._____

5._____

Q8.2 In the two pictures below, one shows the correct lifting method, and the other does not. Identify which is which and explain why.

Q8.3 Using the words provided, complete these sentences about fitness when working on a yard.

| fit | co-ordinated | safely | stresses | strains |

Physical fitness is necessary to work _____ on the yard. A _____ person is likely to be

stronger, more _____ and capable of carrying out yard work than someone who is not. This

makes the work more efficiently achieved with fewer possibilities of _____ and _____.

Q8.4 Explain why this is the best way to carry a filled haynet.

Q8.5 Add the missing words to describe how to fill a haynet.

| three | one | slide | clean |

With two people, _____ hands hold open the net, whilst one hand fills.

If only _____ person, lie the net on a _____ surface. Lift open the top side and

_____ the hay in.

Q8.6 (a) How is a haynet weighed?
(b) Estimate the average weight of hay and haylage in the haynet sizes below.

(a) _____

(b)

SMALL HAYNET	
SMALL HAYNET WITH HAYLAGE	
LARGE HAYNET	
LARGE HAYNET WITH HAYLAGE	

Q8.7 Tying up a haynet. Describe what's happening in this sequence.

Q8.8 List three potential dangers to the horse when using haynets.

1._____

2._____

3._____

Q8.9 Prompted by the key words below, explain the benefits of using haynets.

WEIGHT

_____

SOAKING

_____

WASTE

_____

HYGIENIC

_____

WORMS

_____

9 HORSE HEALTH

Q9.1 On the horse below, label the signs of good health.

Q9.2 List all the signs of poor health that you know. The drawings below hint at some of the answers.

Q9.3 Tell-tale signs in the stable and field provide indications as to the horse's health. Complete the table to explain what to look for in regard to the topics listed.

	STABLE	FIELD
FEED		
HAY		
DROPPINGS		
WATER		
BED		

Q9.4 Morning inspections include a quick look at the horse to check that he is in basic good health before he is watered, hayed and fed. List the things you would look for in this first quick check of the morning.

_____

_____

_____

_____

_____

_____

Q9.5 If, during your morning check, you felt that the horse was unwell, what would you do?

_____

_____

Q9.6 How do you check that a horse is warm enough?

_____

Q9.7 Listed below are statements about why you should report ill-health to a senior member of staff. Decide whether you think that they are TRUE or FALSE.

Senior staff have more experience and can therefore make a more knowledgeable assessment.

Senior staff have probably known the horse for longer and may have more information on the horse's medical history.

A decision can be made quickly to give medical attention or to call the vet.

The groom has a responsibility for the welfare of the horse in their care.

Horses are better at healing themselves without our interference.

Q9.8 List five stable management rules which help to maintain horses in good health.

1. _____

2. _____

3. _____

4. _____

5. _____

Q10.1 Put these instincts in order of natural priority for the horse and then match them up with explanations of each by writing 1, 2 or 3 beside the explanations.

NOURISH   PROCREATE   SURVIVE

| 1 → | 2 → | 3 |

Seek fresh clean water [ ]

Eat well on good grazing [ ]

Fight to stay alive if cornered [ ]

Graze [ ]

Mares come into season in spring/summer [ ]

Foals are naturally born at the time of spring grass growth [ ]

Only one stallion per herd [ ]

Run away from danger [ ]

Pass on dominant genes [ ]

Choose a variety of grasses [ ]

Remain with the herd [ ]

Nomadic [ ]

Q10.2 Each picture illustrates one of the horse's natural characteristics. Can you label the drawings appropriately?

Q10.3 Match the sound to the description by drawing a line from one to the other.

WHINNY	Anger, fear, pain if mare/gelding. If from a stallion, possibly also excitement or a challenge
SCREAM	Long-distance call to gain attention, e.g. a horse on his own in a field calling to companions
SNORT	High-pitched – excitement/tension, e.g. heard from mare and foal during weaning
NEIGH	High-pitched, short sound, e.g. mare in season
SIGH	Frequent, quick nasal blows to draw in as much scent as possible, e.g. sniffing droppings of an unfamiliar horse
SNORING/ GROANING	Short, sharp sound of fear, e.g. a young horse taken on his own into an indoor school for the first time
SQUEAL	Soft, breathy sound of recognition, e.g. of a person or a horse
BLOW	Contentment, e.g. during chewing
NICKER	Heard during sleep

Q10.4 The horse expresses himself through body language. Describe the body language/physical signs for each state, and include any special handling required, apart from normal awareness.

INTERPRETATION	BODY LANGUAGE
HAPPY	
INQUISITIVE	
PLAYFUL	
ANXIOUS	
GRUMPY	
VERY GRUMPY	

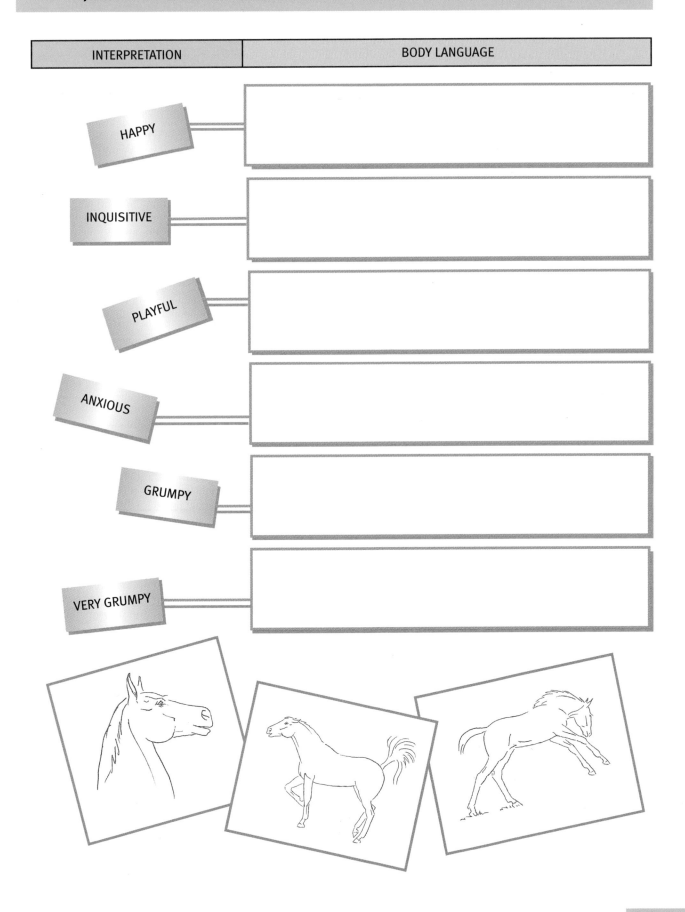

Q10.5 As a groom, you need certain qualities and know-how when handling and riding horses. Read the list below and then fit each letter appropriately into the table. If there are any traits/actions that you feel are inappropriate, underline them in red.

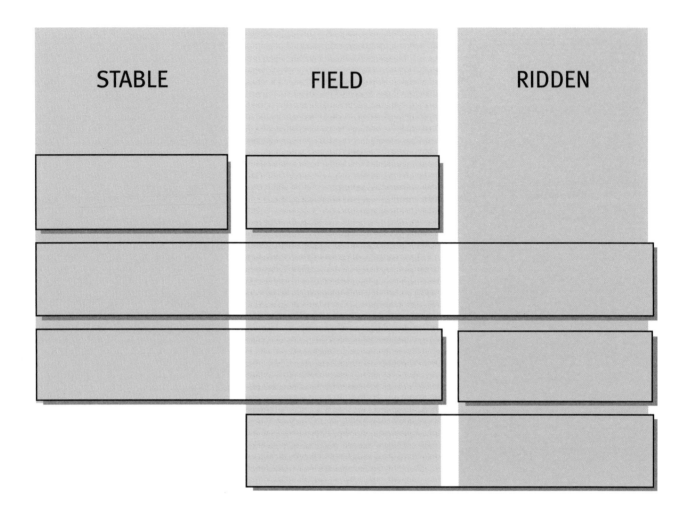

STABLE   FIELD   RIDDEN

(a) Be patient.
(b) Show understanding.
(c) Never enter the stable if the horse's hind legs are facing the door.
(d) Always ensure that the horse is facing the door before you enter the stable.
(e) Whenever possible, lead from the left side.
(f) If leading on the road, lead from the right, putting yourself between the horse and traffic.
(g) Be quick-tempered.
(h) Never carry a bucket of food into a field with more than one horse in it.
(i) Approach the horse at his shoulder.
(j) Be decisive.
(k) Ride with quiet confidence.
(l) Have authority.
(m) Tie the horse up when working around him.
(n) Risk assess each situation.
(o) Ride with clarity and sympathy.
(p) Always move the horse around so that you are working in a safe space.
(q) Give clear aids/instructions.

Q10.6 Some horses can be difficult to catch in the field. List at least two methods that could be used and state how they relate to the horse's natural instincts and characteristics.

1. _____

_____

_____

2. _____

_____

Q10.7 If you are unsure how to handle a horse that shows negative feelings, what should you do?

_____

_____

_____

Q10.8 Describe the possible signs of danger in the horse's expression and action when ridden.

	EXPRESSION
EARS	
EYES	
NOSTRILS	
LEGS	
WHOLE BODY	
TAIL	

11 BASIC GRASSLAND CARE

Q11.1 The table below lists the items that should be inspected in a field check. In each box write what you would look for and why.

FENCING	
WATER	
GATE	
SHELTER	
GRAZING	
GROUND	
POISONOUS PLANTS	

Q11.2 Name each type of fencing and state whether it is suitable for fields with horses.

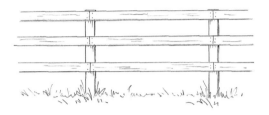

_____

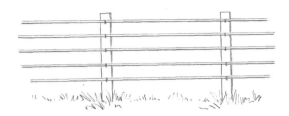

_____

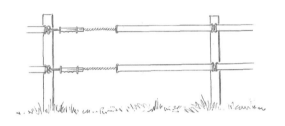

_____

_____

_____

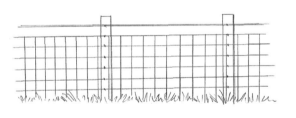

_____

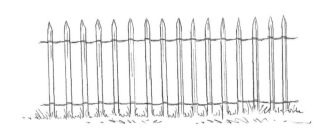

_____

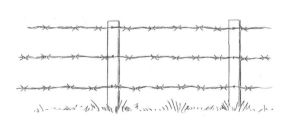

_____

Q11.3 The picture below shows a horse-sick field. Label the key factors that point to this condition.

_____

_____

_____

_____

_____

_____

_____

Q11.4 How can the undesirable field issues outlined in Q11.3 be avoided/remedied?

_____

_____

_____

_____

_____

_____

_____

_____

Q11.5 Why are droppings removed from fields?

_____

_____

Q11.6 What is the minimum recommended size of field to sustain (a) a horse (b) a pony?

_____

Q11.7 If you had five ponies in a field, how many piles of hay would you put out and why?

_____

_____

Q11.8 This cartoon strip shows the correct procedure for turning a horse out into a field. Describe each picture.

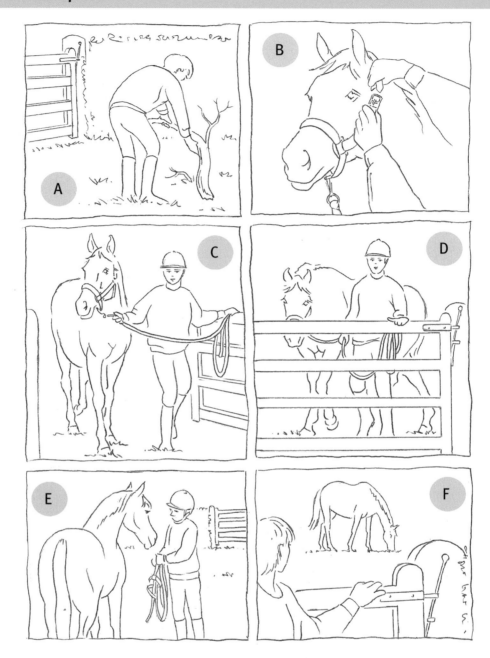

A _____

B _____

C _____

D _____

E _____

F _____

Q11.9 This cartoon strip shows what NOT to do when bringing a horse in from the field. List all the dangers/problems/hazards or poor practice that you can see.

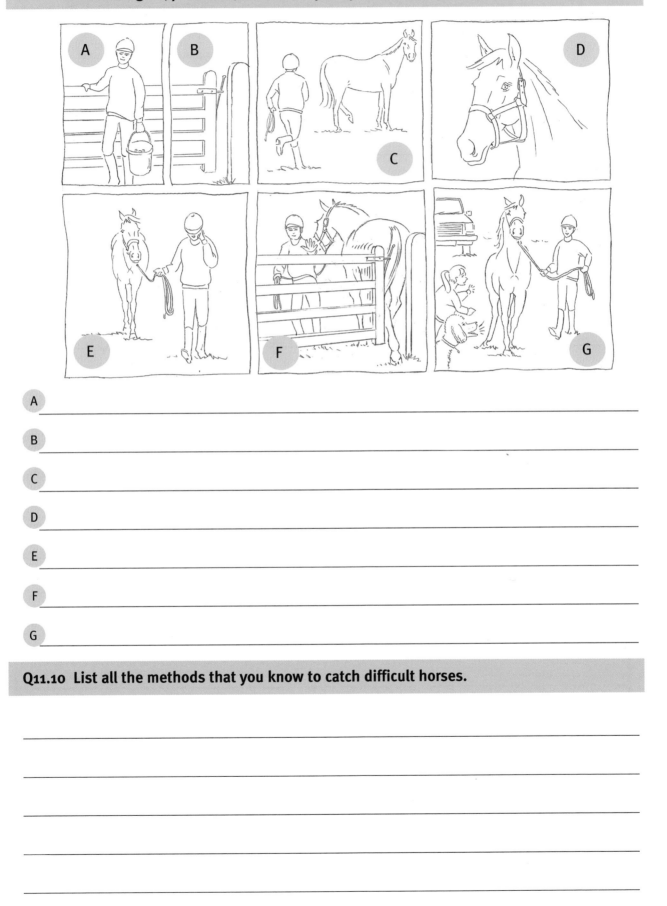

A _____

B _____

C _____

D _____

E _____

F _____

G _____

Q11.10 List all the methods that you know to catch difficult horses.

_____

_____

_____

_____

_____

12 WATERING AND FEEDING

Q12.1 Assessing hay. Complete the table with descriptions of what you would look for when checking the quality of hay.

	GOOD QUALITY HAY	BAD QUALITY HAY
SMELL		
COLOUR		
GRASSES		
DUST		
FEEL		

Q12.2 Hay varies in quality at different times of the year and depending on whether there was a good harvest the previous year. We know our ideal of what we would like. Now state what is acceptable, and absolutely not acceptable.

ACCEPTABLE	NOT ACCEPTABLE

Q12.3 Circle the statements that indicate good quality haylage.

Plastic wrapping is pierced

Good grasses

Sweet smelling

Dusty

Higher moisture content than hay

Barbed wire found in the bale

Soggy mulch

White areas of mould

Separates when handled

Golden stems

A few docks

Q12.4 List five dangers arising from feeding poor quality hay/haylage.

_____

_____

_____

_____

_____

Q12.5 List the rules of good feeding, prompted by the key words below.

AMOUNT	
QUALITY	
HYGIENE	
ROUTINE	
CHANGES	
SUCCULENT	
FIBRE	
LITTLE AND OFTEN	
EXERCISE	
WATER	

Q12.6 List the rules of watering.

1. _____

2. _____

3. _____

4. _____

5. _____

Q12.7 The pictures show different methods of watering horses at grass. In the boxes, write the advantages and disadvantages of each.

	ADVANTAGE	DISADVANTAGE

Q12.8 Describe one method of feeding horses in the field.

_____

_____

_____

_____

Q12.9 Think of a seasonal feeding plan for a grass-kept pony in light work and write the percentages in the table.

	HAY%	CONCENTRATES%
SUMMER		
AUTUMN AND SPRING		
WINTER		

Q12.10 Choosing from the feeds and forages below, circle the ones that you feel are suitable for a stabled horse or pony in light work.

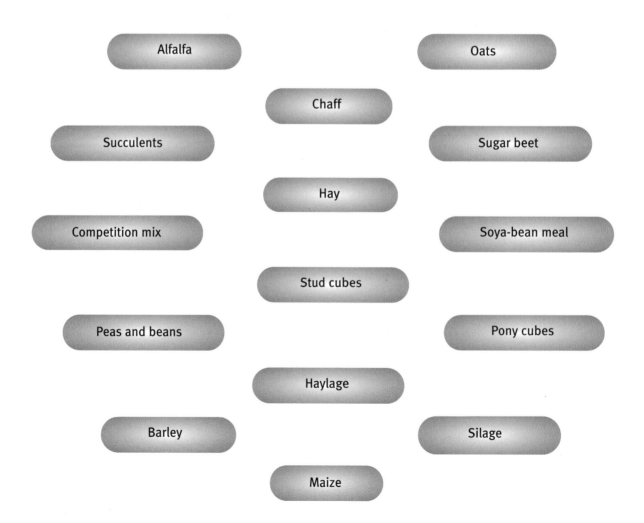

Alfalfa

Oats

Chaff

Succulents

Sugar beet

Hay

Competition mix

Soya-bean meal

Stud cubes

Peas and beans

Pony cubes

Haylage

Barley

Silage

Maize

Q12.11 Complete this chart of feed percentages relative to workload.

WORKLOAD	DEFINITION	ROUGHAGE%	CONCENTRATE%
MAINTENANCE			
LIGHT			
MEDIUM			
HARD			

Q12.12 Work out a daily feeding plan for a 16hh riding club horse who is stabled and in light work. Assume that he is neither a poor doer nor a good doer, but he can become a little fizzy when ridden, which scares his owner.

13 GENERAL KNOWLEDGE

Q13.1 Circle the clothing that you feel is appropriate for working in all weathers on the yard.

Long-sleeved top	Baggy trousers	Waterproof coat
Jewellery	Trainers	Jodhpurs
Flip-flops	Comfortable, well-fitting trousers	Sturdy boots

Q13.2 Circle all the fire precautions that you can see in this picture of a yard.

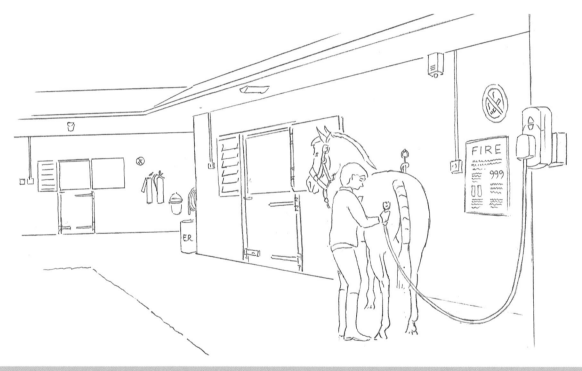

Q13.3 What do the letters below stand for when there is an accident involving a person?

A _____

P _____

A _____

CH _____

Q13.5 When assessing an unconscious casualty, what will the letters A, B and C help you to remember?

A_____ B_____ C_____

Q13.5 Here we see a casualty who is unconscious, but with good respiration and pulse, being put into the recovery position. Describe what is happening in each picture.

A _____

B _____

C _____

D _____

E _____

F _____

G _____

H _____

Q13.6 List five safety rules for riding in a class.

_____

_____

_____

_____

_____

Q13.7 Riding on the road. Here we see one rider hacking and one leading. List ten rules and good practices employed when taking horses on a public highway, as depicted in the drawings.

1 _____

2 _____

3 _____

4 _____

5 _____

6 _____

7 _____

8 _____

9 _____

10 _____

Q13.8 Complete the aims of The British Horse Society from the key words.

| Training and Education | Breeding | Protection | Welfare |

_____

_____

_____

_____

_____

_____

_____

_____

Q14.1 From the selection of pictures below and right, tick the two that show how to correctly lead a tacked-up horse. Explain what is right and wrong with each of the drawings.

1 _____

_____

_____

_____

2 _____

_____

3 _____

_____

_____

4 _____

_____

_____

5 _____

_____

6 _____

_____

Q14.2 Before mounting, certain checks should be carried out on the horse and the tack. Label and describe the checks that you would make.

Q14.3 How can you estimate the correct length for your stirrups before mounting?

_____

Q14.4 Correct mounting sequence. Describe what's happening in each picture.

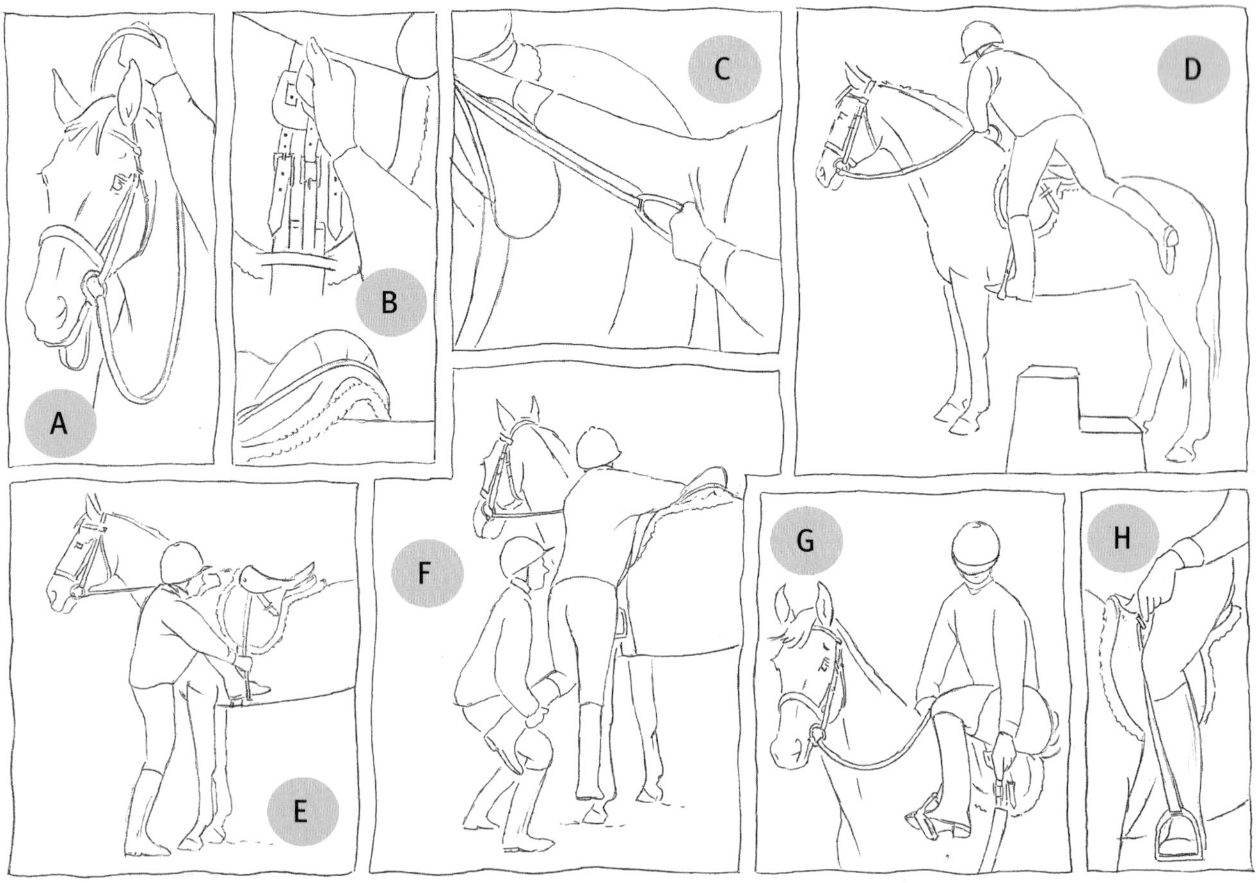

A _____

B _____

C _____

D _____

_____

E _____

_____

F _____

_____

G _____

H _____

Q14.5 From the pictures below, identify the correct positioning of stirrup and leather when ridden, and label the mistakes in the other pictures.

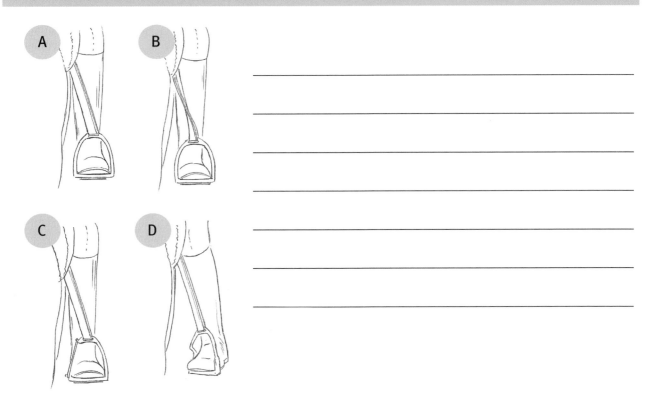

_____

_____

_____

_____

_____

_____

_____

Q14.6 Mark the faults that you can spot with the horse's tack.

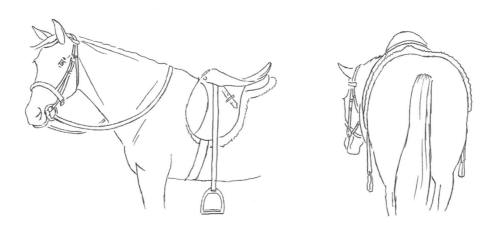

Q14.7 Add a sentence to each label to describe how to hold the reins correctly.

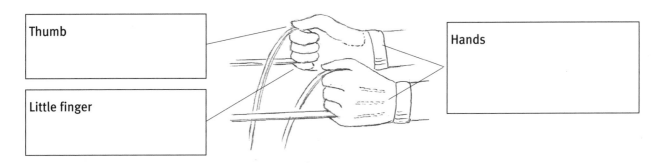

Thumb

Little finger

Hands

Q14.8 Describe the differences between these two images, which show good and bad position.

Q14.9 Fill in the gaps to describe how to change over a short whip correctly.

Having changed the rein and _____ the horse, place both _____ into the_____

hand. Using the _____ hand, pull the whip through to the inside. Replace _____ rein in each

hand. Position the _____ correctly over the _____.

Q14.10 Circle the correct sequence of footfalls in walk, trot and canter. In each case, the first step has been circled for you.

WALK

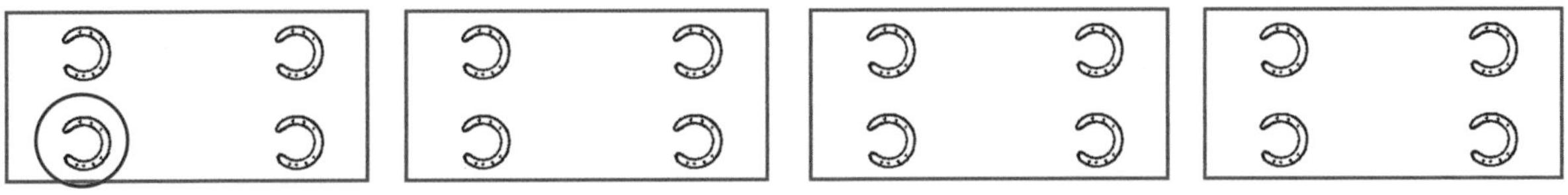

TROT

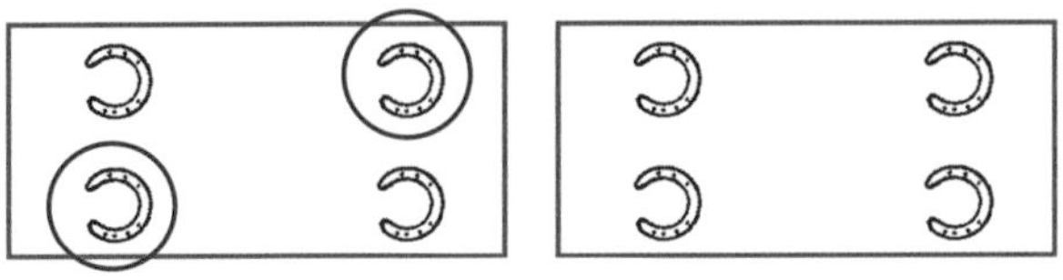

CANTER (Left)

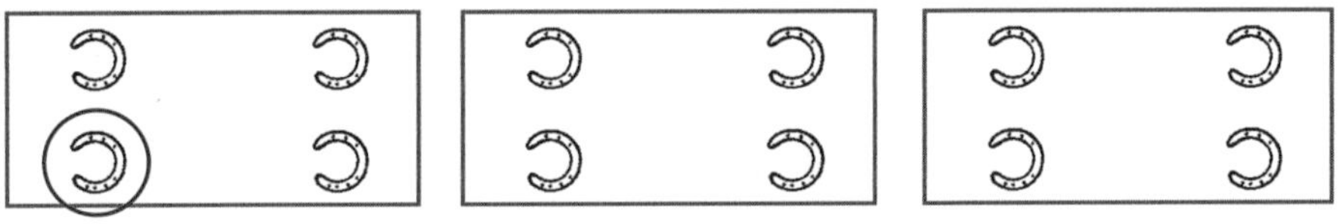

CANTER (Right)

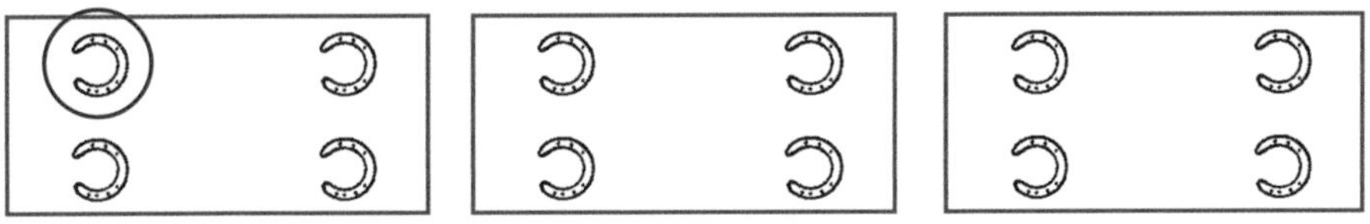

Q14.11 Write down as many of the responsibilities associated with lead file as you can think of.

_____

_____

_____

_____

_____

_____

Q14.12 List the natural and artificial aids, and how you would apply them.

_____

_____

_____

_____

_____

_____

_____

_____

_____

_____

_____

_____

_____

Q14.13 Fill in the gaps to complete the description of how you would recognise the correct trot diagonal, and how it helps the horse for the rider to be on the correct one.

When riding on the left rein, the rider should be on the _____ trot diagonal. This can be recognised

by looking at the horse's outside (right) _____, and with more experience, the rider will be able to

_____ whether they are right or wrong. When looking at the outside shoulder, the rider should be

_____ as the shoulder moves back, and _____ as it travels forwards. Being on the correct

diagonal helps the horse's _____, and the co-ordination of the rider's _____.

Q14.14 Draw a different change of rein on each of these arena plans.

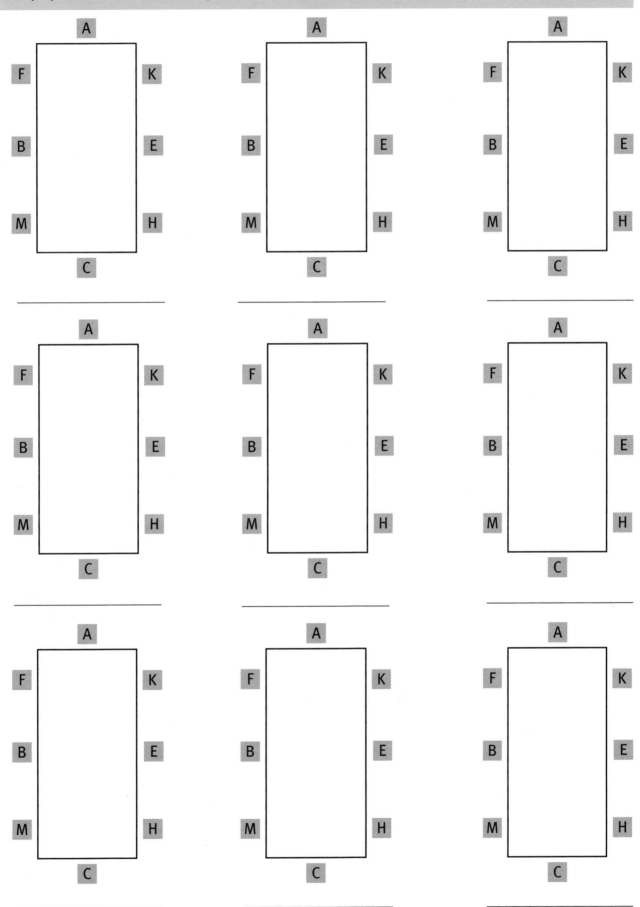

1 GROOMING

HOOF PICK

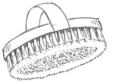
BODY BRUSH

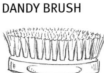
DANDY BRUSH

PLASTIC CURRY COMB

RUBBER CURRY COMB

METAL CURRY COMB

Q1.1

A HOOF PICK – for cleaning out the underside of the horse's hoof.
B BODY BRUSH – removes dried sweat and dust from the clipped, stabled horse.
C DANDY BRUSH – removes dried sweat and mud from the field-kept, unclipped horse.
D PLASTIC CURRY COMB – removes dried sweat and mud from the unclipped, field-kept horse. It can also be used to clean the body brush.
E RUBBER CURRY COMB – excellent at removing winter coat during the spring, mud, sweat and scurf. Used in circular motions.
F METAL CURRY COMB – only ever used to clean brushes.
G SWEAT SCRAPER – removes excess water on the horse's body when the horse has been washed down. Only used on large muscle areas.
H MANE/TAIL COMB – used to pull mane and tail, and as an aid when plaiting.
I SPONGES – one for eyes and nose, one for dock and sheath/udders.
J MASSAGE PAD – improves circulation. Only used on large muscle areas.
K STABLE RUBBER – gives a finishing polish by removing residual dust.
L HOOF OIL – light oil to give shine and condition to hooves.

SWEAT SCRAPER

MANE/TAIL COMB

Q1.2

Health – remove dust, sweat, dead skin, loose hair.
Condition – muscle tone.
Prevention of disease – helps to prevent skin diseases and parasites.
Appearance – neat, tidy and attractive.
Checking for new heat/swelling – quick and efficient treatment of new injuries.
Cleanliness – hygiene prevents sores.

SPONGES

Q1.3

Brushing off:
1 Tie up the horse.
2 Pick out the feet.
3 Brush the body.
4 Sponge eyes, nose and dock.

MASSAGE PAD

Q1.4

Quartering:
1 Tie up the horse.
2 Pick out the feet.
3 Undo and secure the rug fastenings.
4 Fold the front of the rug back.
5 Brush the front of the body and mane.
6 Fold the rear of the rug forward.
7 Brush the back of the horse.
8 Secure the rug.
9 Clean the tail.
10 Sponge eyes, nose and dock.

STABLE RUBBER
HOOF OIL

Q1.5

Horse not tied.
Door not shut.
Picking up hind foot incorrectly.
Using metal curry comb on horse's body.
Sitting on the floor to apply hoof oil.
Front straps undone, rest of the rug still fastened.
Standing directly behind the horse to clean the dock.
Number of people (four) in the stable!

Q1.6

1 Start the bandage with the end flap out.
2 Fold flap over.
3 Roll bandage over flap.
4 Wrap evenly all the way down to the base of tail bone.
5 Return back up the tail.
6 Tie tapes on the side.
7 Fold the last wrap over the bow.

Q1.7

Untie. Bandage. Slide.

2 CLOTHING

Q2.1

New Zealand   Stable   Cooler/Sweat Rug

NEW ZEALAND – A waterproof turn-out rug used during
inclement weather. Varying weights.
STABLE – A duvet-filled rug used for the stabled horse.
Varying weights.
COOLER/SWEAT RUG – This rug wicks away moisture
from a wet horse, either caused by work, a bath or rain,
whilst keeping the horse warm.

Q2.2

1 Securely tie up the horse.
2 Place the rug over the horse's withers.
3 Fasten the front straps.
4 Unfold the rug.
5 Secure the surcingle straps, crossing them underneath
   the horse's stomach.
6 Fasten the leg straps/pull the tail over the fillet string.

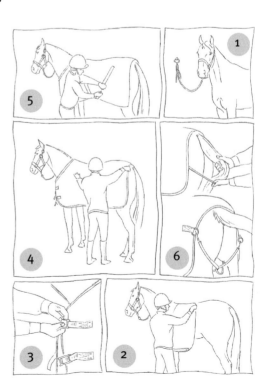

Q2.3

CORRECT FIT OF:
Withers
Chest
Shoulders
Depth
Length
Fastenings

Q2.4

POOR FIT OF:
Withers
Chest
Shoulders
Depth
Length
Fastenings

Q2.5

1 Rug with leg straps fastened to the same side, having just been put on.
2 One leg strap fastened correctly around one leg.
3 Both leg straps fastened, having looped the second through the first.
4 (Incorrect) The leg straps are done up, without having looped one through the other.
5 (Incorrect) The leg straps are fastened on opposite sides.

Q2.6

True
False
True
True
True

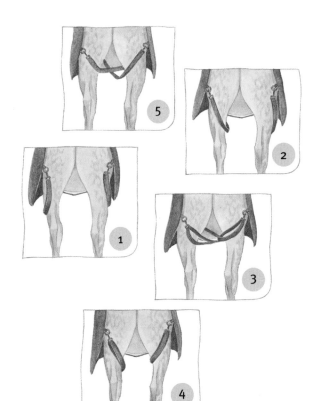

Q2.7

STABLE	NEW ZEALAND	COOLER
Tough	Usually has leg straps	Wicks away moisture from the horse
Non-waterproof	Waterproof	Maintains warmth whilst allowing the horse to cool down
Durable	Duvet-like filling	Usually has a fillet string
Some have tail flaps	Some have tail flaps	
Duvet-like filling	Durable	
	Tough	

3 SADDLERY

Q3.1

Labelled saddle.

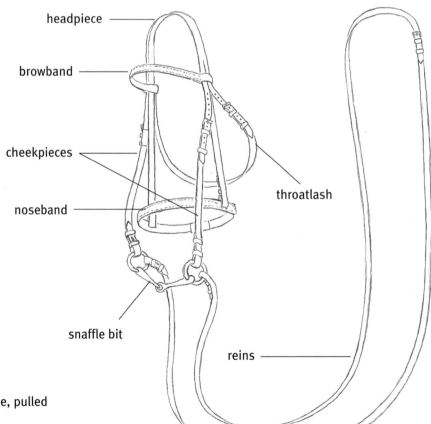

point pocket

thigh roll

knee roll

girth straps

buckle guard

pommel

seat

waist

stud

cantle

skirt

panel lining

saddle flap

cantle

panel

girth straps

gullet

Q3.2

Labelled snaffle bridle.

headpiece

browband

cheekpieces

throatlash

noseband

snaffle bit

reins

Q3.3

Size is appropriate.
Pommel and cantle level.
Numnah even under saddle, pulled
up into gullet.
Even bearing surface from behind.

Q3.4

RUNNING MARTINGALE
Neckstrap joins martingale where neck meets chest.
One hand's width between neckstrap and wither.

STANDING MARTINGALE
Correct length measured by running the martingale up the gullet, under the jaw and to the noseband.
One hand's width between neckstrap and wither.

Q3.5

Place over head on horse's neck.
Attach to girth.
Attach straps to D-rings.

Q3.6

DIRTY GIRTH	Girth galls
THIN STIRRUP LEATHERS	Leathers could snap while riding
WORN STITCHING ON STIRRUP LEATHERS	Leathers could split while riding
DIRTY NUMNAH	Saddle sores
WORN STITCHES ON GIRTH STRAPS	Girth could come undone while riding

Q3.7

1 Tack collected and positioned safely.
2 Headcollar on and the groomed horse is tied up.
3 Rope looped through string; headcollar is fastened around the horse's neck.
4 Bridle is put on by sliding the bit gently into the mouth, lifting into position and sliding the headpiece over the ears.
5 The noseband is fastened and the reins twisted through the throatlash.
6 Headcollar is replaced and the horse retied.
7 The numnah is put on.
8 The saddle is positioned, pulling the numnah into the gullet of the saddle and sliding into place.
9 Moving to the offside of the horse, the girth is taken off the top of the saddle, letting it hang down.
10 The saddle is girthed up so that it remains in position, but not tight enough to mount. The buckle guards are pulled down.

Q3.8

1 Tie the horse up.
2 Undo the girth, move to the offside and place the girth over the saddle.
3 Remove the saddle, lifting it up and over.
4 Safely position the saddle out of the way.
5 Untie the horse and thread the rope through the baler cord.
6 Tie the headcollar around the horse's neck.
7 Undo the noseband and throatlash.
8 Remove the bridle, being careful not to knock the horse's teeth.
9 Replace the headcollar and retie.
10 Put the tack away neatly.

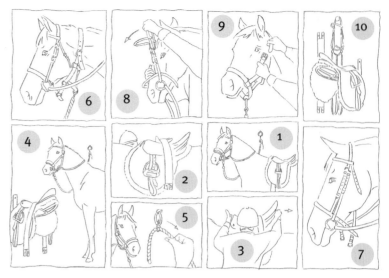

Q3.9

(a) Pony, cob, full and sometimes extra full.

(b) Place the numnah on the horse's back a little further forward than the position of the saddle. Place the saddle on top and pull the numnah up into the gullet of the saddle. Slide both saddle and numnah back into the correct position; this aids the hair to lie flat. Attach the numnah to the saddle by the loops usually positioned for the girth straps and girth.

Q3.10

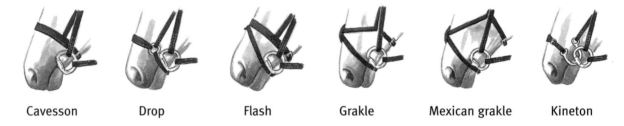

| Cavesson | Drop | Flash | Grakle | Mexican grakle | Kineton |

CAVESSON – aesthetic – buckle under the jaw.

DROP – prevents the horse from opening his mouth and evading the bit – fastened under the bit with the buckle positioned so that it is not in the way of the bit or the lips.

FLASH – prevents the horse opening his mouth or crossing the jaw.

GRAKLE – action like a flash, but acts over a wider area and point of pressure on the front of the nose. Both buckles do up under the jaw.

MEXICAN GRAKLE – as the grakle, but fitted over the projecting cheek bones, rather than under, therefore more pressure.

KINETON – when the reins are pulled, pressure is exerted on the nose also. Fits over the nose and under the bit.

Q3.11

(a) Warm water – cleans the tack – removes sweat and grime.
    EITHER Oil – supples and waterproofs.
    OR Saddle soap – supples, waterproofs and shines.

(b) Stripping tack, preferably weekly, enables every part of the tack to have a thorough clean and for the stitching and leather to be checked for safety. If this does not happen, areas that are not regularly oiled and soaped are likely to crack and break.

4 HANDLING

Q4.1

Stable door left open.
Tools left lying around.
Shavings bag on the floor.
Grooming kit left in middle of the walkway.
Light switch near stable.
Power point for radio near stable.
Rugs left untidily on the floor.

Q4.2

SAFETY. Of horse and groom.
RISK ASSESSMENTS. Think of potential problems as a result of an action. Try to avoid the risks. Learn to risk-assess all aspects of working with horses.
RESPECT. Respect for the horse – they are large animals. Horses must have respect for their grooms. The groom must be assertive and fair. He/she must be a leader to the horse. Reward when good (positive reinforcement), reprimand when unruly.
COMMUNICATION. For the horse to be capable of understanding what we want, we must communicate successfully. Voice and body language should reinforce each other.
DISCIPLINE. Following a routine, consistent commands and principles produce a disciplined horse.
ROUTINE. Horses thrive on routine. Try to maintain a daily routine.

Q4.3

Prepare the headcollar ready to use by unravelling the lead rope if rolled, ensuring that the noseband is done up and that the headpiece is undone. Approach the horse at his shoulder. Standing just in front of the shoulder, facing the horse's head, lift the noseband over the nose. Position the headpiece over the poll, avoiding the ears, and fasten the buckle. To check the fit, the noseband should fit two fingers' width below the projecting cheek bone and with two fingers' width between the noseband and the face.

Q4.4

(a) Baler cord, non-slip floor, no hazards for the horse in the area.
(b)

Q4.5

The equine industry requires employees who are efficient and safe. Working with horses is hard, physical work, but if a routine is worked to and everybody knows their role within a team, it can be fun and rewarding.

5 HORSE HUSBANDRY

Q5.1

BEDDING	STRAW	SHAVINGS	HEMP	PAPER	RUBBER MATTING
EXPENSIVE	Depends on season	Yes	Yes	Yes	Initial cost
EDIBLE	Yes	No	No	No	No
EASY STORAGE	Need barn	Yes	Yes	Yes	N/A
EASY DISPOSAL	Yes	Not always – long time to rot	Yes	Not always – depends	Yes – less waste
DUSTY	Possibly	Possibly	No	No	No
COMFORT	Yes	Yes	Can have sharp shards	Yes	No
CLEAN	Yes	Yes	Yes	No	Always use with bedding

Q5.2

Stale/urinate – horses prefer to urinate on bedding/grass rather than on a hard floor; lie down – for rest and relaxation; roll – for enjoyment or if sweaty/wet. Warmth and protection – to ensure horse stays warm in winter and to protect him from injury.

Q5.3

Although types of bedding vary, maintenance is fairly similar. They are all generally mucked out once per day and skipped out every time you enter the stable. Day beds tend to be thinner, with the bedding thrown up into the banks. More bedding may be added to night beds so that the horse has a thicker bed in which to lie down at night. Banks are built to preclude draughts and to prevent the horse from becoming cast.

Q5.4

ADVANTAGES	DISADVANTAGES
DAILY MUCKING OUT	
• Clean, dry bed • Horses' feet are likely to remain clean and dry	• Labour intensive
DEEP LITTERING	
• Quick to manage, on a daily basis • Offers a warm, thick, non-slip base to the bed	• Labour intensive when dug out weekly • Particular attention needs to be paid to the health of the foot as more prone to induce thrush

Q5.5

1 Remove the horse from the stable or tie up securely.
2 Remove the water buckets.
3 Remove the droppings.
4 Remove the wet area, sorting it from the clean.
5 Throw all the bedding up onto one bank (rotated daily).
6 Sweep the floor.
7 Lay the bed.
8 Replace the freshly filled water buckets.

Q5.6

SKIPPING OUT – The quick and efficient removal of droppings.
SETTING FAIR – Tidy up – skip out, create a neat bed, sweep around the stable, check water.

Q5.7

Three heaps:
• One well rotted and ready to be taken away as manure.
• One in the process of rotting.
• One in use. This must be maintained daily to prevent unnecessary spread of the area.
All should be built square and kept well trodden down to keep the air out, minimising fire risk.

Q5.8

Wheelbarrow the wrong way around.
Tossing muck from behind/underneath the horse.
Other tools left inside the stable.
Haynet on the floor.

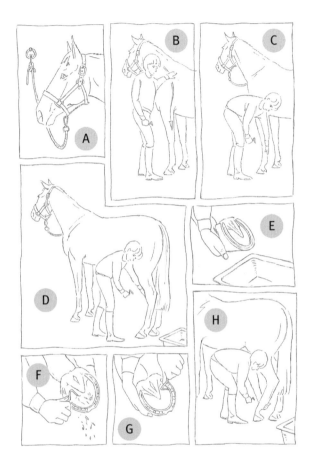

6 THE FOOT AND SHOEING

Q6.1

A Horse tied up securely.
B Start at the front and run the hand down the neck, shoulder and foreleg.
C For the front leg, run the hand down the back of the leg.
D For the back leg, run the hand down the front of the leg. Therefore the arm bends in the direction of the leg.
E The leg is held into the body and supported underneath the hoof and pastern.
F Pick out the feet using a downward movement with the hoof pick. Start at the heel and run down each lateral cleft, avoiding the soft, sensitive frog.
G Clean out the sole area, checking the shoe at the same time.
H Gently place the foot on the ground.

Q6.2

Using a water brush, clean the outside of the hooves. Pick up each foot in turn and gently scrub the underside of each hoof. Once the feet are dry, oil inside and out using a light oil.

Q6.3

Recently shod – shod one or two weeks ago.
In need of shoeing – the foot requires attention.
Risen clenches – as the toe grows, it takes the shoe forwards causing the clenches to rise.
Sprung shoe – the shoe is not flat on the horse's foot; it may be pulled away from the foot and be bent.
Loose shoe – there is movement of the shoe when examined.
Cast shoe – the shoe has come off.
Worn thin – thin, wafer-like shoes that may actually snap.
Long feet – many horses grow more at the toe than at the heel and therefore give the impression of long toes.
Overgrown foot – growth over the sides of the shoe.

Q6.4

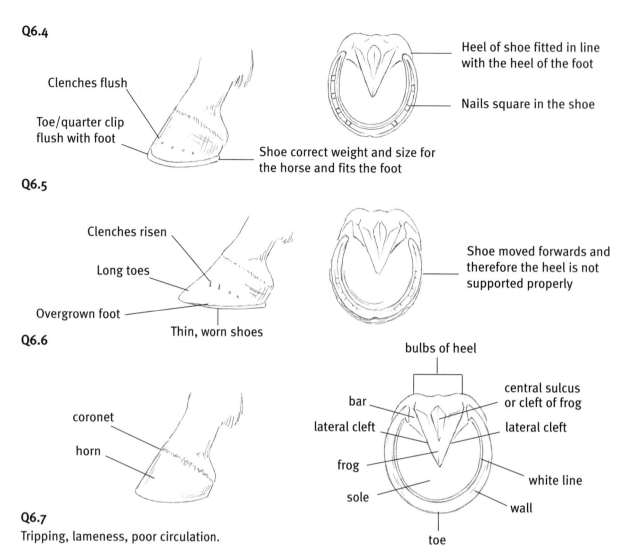

Clenches flush

Toe/quarter clip flush with foot

Shoe correct weight and size for the horse and fits the foot

Heel of shoe fitted in line with the heel of the foot

Nails square in the shoe

Q6.5

Clenches risen

Long toes

Overgrown foot

Thin, worn shoes

Shoe moved forwards and therefore the heel is not supported properly

Q6.6

coronet

horn

bulbs of heel

bar

central sulcus or cleft of frog

lateral cleft

lateral cleft

frog

white line

sole

wall

toe

Q6.7

Tripping, lameness, poor circulation.

7 ANATOMY AND HANDLING

Q7.1

A Forelock	I Point of elbow	Q Stifle
B Muzzle	J Chestnut	R Back
C Jugular groove	K Pastern	S Withers
D Forearm	L Hock	T Crest
E Knee	M Point of buttock	U Poll
F Coronet	N Dock	V Shoulder
G Hoof	O Point of hip	
H Fetlock	P Croup	

Q7.2

BAY	Brown (any shade) body with black mane, tail and legs.
GREY	White/grey all over.
CHESTNUT	Chestnut all over.
BLACK	Black all over.
BROWN	Brown all over.
DUN	Sandy body with black mane, tail and legs.
PALOMINO	Sandy body with cream/white mane and tail.
PIEBALD	Black and white all over.
SKEWBALD	Black, brown and white, or just brown and white all over.
SPOTTED	White with black spots or dark with white spots.
ROAN	Base colour of chestnut, bay, or grey with flecks of white all over.

Q7.3

GREY

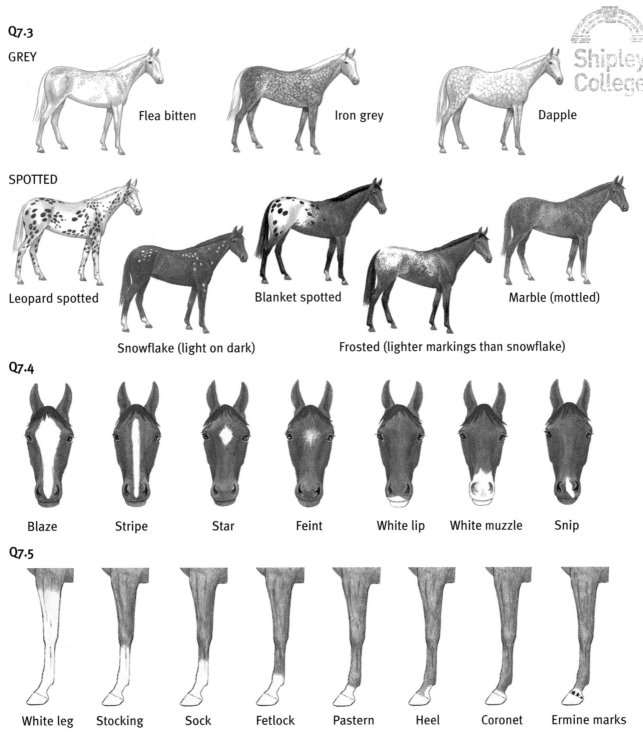

Flea bitten

Iron grey

Dapple

SPOTTED

Leopard spotted

Blanket spotted

Marble (mottled)

Snowflake (light on dark)

Frosted (lighter markings than snowflake)

Q7.4

Blaze   Stripe   Star   Feint   White lip   White muzzle   Snip

Q7.5

White leg   Stocking   Sock   Fetlock   Pastern   Heel   Coronet   Ermine marks

Q7.6

Mealy muzzle	Lighter around the muzzle
Toad eye	Lighter around the eye
Dorsal line	Darker stripe down the spine
Zebra markings	Stripes on the legs
Whorl	Circular ring of hair with a definite centre
Injury marking	Area of trauma identified from the white hairs which grow at the site of injury

Q7.7

DIFFERENCES
The horse can be anxious about treatments and not about inspections.
The inspection is usually carried out on hard, level ground and the horse must be standing squarely.
Treatment may be in a loosebox.
Stand slightly forward of the horse, but to the side for an inspection, so the viewer can see the whole horse.

SIMILARITIES
Always on the same side as the person treating or inspecting the horse. This way you are aware if they are likely to do anything which will make the horse react. Try to keep the horse calm. A bridle may be necessary to help with control.

Q7.8

Hat and gloves.
Whip in left hand.
Bridle.
Holding the reins correctly.
Led at the horse's shoulder.
Freedom for the horse to move his head naturally, but enough control to keep the horse straight.

Q7.9

In front of the horse.
Facing the horse.
Shouting at the horse.
Waving the whip.
No hat/gloves.
Headcollar, not bridle.

Q7.10

In walk, turn the horse away from you, so that you are on the outside of the horse. This gives you greater control and prevents your feet from being trodden on. Walk a comfortable size turn for the horse.

8 HEALTH AND SAFETY

Q8.1

Carrying tack.
Saddling a large horse.
Lifting a filled haynet.
Moving small bales of hay/straw.
Lifting up a heavy wheelbarrow.

Q8.2

Bad:	Good:
Legs straight.	Keep back straight.
Object far away.	Get close to the object to be lifted.
Lifting like this will place strain on the back.	Bend knees and gain good purchase on the object.
	During the lift, take the strain on the legs, not the back.

Q8.3

Physical fitness is necessary to work safely on the yard. A fit person is likely to be stronger, more co-ordinated and capable of carrying out yard work than someone who is not. This makes the work more efficiently achieved with fewer possibilities of stresses and strains.

Q8.4

Straight back.
The haynet is carried in the centre of the back with the weight of the net running through the legs and feet.

Q8.5

With two people, three hands hold open the net, whilst one hand fills.
If only one person, lie the net on a clean surface. Lift open the top side and slide the hay in.

Q8.6

Spring balance.

Small haynet	2–3lbs (1–1.5kg)
Small haynet with haylage	4–5lbs (2–2.5kg)
Large haynet	6–9lbs (3–4.5kg)
Large haynet with haylage	12–15lbs (6–7.5kg)

Q8.7

Loop the drawstring through the tie-ring or string.

Pull the net up to the ring.

Thread the drawstring through the bottom of the net . . .

. . . and pull the bottom up as high as possible.

Secure with a quick-release knot.

Turn the net over so that the knot is on the underside.

Q8.8

The knot is pulled loose by the horse, releasing the net onto the floor.
The net is tied too low and the horse's legs/feet become caught in the net.
The haynet can become tangled up with the teeth.

Q8.9

WEIGHT – using a spring balance, it is possible to be very accurate with the amount of hay given.
SOAKING – easy to soak/dampen hay.
WASTE – less wasteful than feeding off the floor.
HYGIENIC – more hygienic than feeding on the floor.
WORMS – less likelihood of transferring worm burden if a stable is used alternately by different horses.

9 HORSE HEALTH

Q9.1

Behaving normally.
Bright, alert, relaxed.
Shiny coat.
Eyes and nose free from discharge.
Standing squarely – sometimes resting a hind leg, but never a foreleg.

+ if in field: grazing, with the herd, looks sound when moves.

Q9.2

Dull, lethargic.
Head down, droopy.
Dull, staring coat.
'Tucked up' – abdomen lifted and hollow flanks.
Not square in stance.
Frequent rolling.

+ if in field: not grazing, away from the herd, lying down for a long period.

Q9.3

STABLE	FIELD
Feed eaten	Feed eaten (if fed in field)
Hay eaten	Hay eaten (if only horse in field in winter with piles of hay)
Droppings normal number (8–12 per day) and consistency (break on landing on the ground)	If in herd, cannot identify individual droppings
Water drunk – not possible to see with automatic waterers unless metered	Can only check consumption if buckets/butt filled manually and only one horse in the field
Normal bed – messy if normally messy, clean if normally clean	N/A

Q9.4

Bright, alert, looking for food.
Normal breathing.
No discharge.
Standing squarely.
Bed and droppings normal.
Hay/feed eaten and water drunk.

Q9.5

Report immediately to a senior member of staff.

Q9.6

Feel the base of the horse's ears.

Q9.7

• Senior staff have more experience and can therefore make a more knowledgeable assessment. TRUE.
• Senior staff have probably known the horse for longer and may have more information on the horse's medical history. TRUE.
• A decision can be made quickly to give medical attention or to call the vet. TRUE.
• The groom has a responsibility for the welfare of the horse in their care. TRUE.
• Horses are better at healing themselves without our interference. FALSE.

Q9.8

Check the horse regularly.
Vaccinate regularly.
Worm regularly.
Feed correctly.
Shoe regularly.
Exercise correctly.
Check that the horse has a safe environment – stable, field, arena.
Keep to the routine.

10 HORSE BEHAVIOUR

Q10.1

1. Survive.	Remain with the herd. 1
2. Nourish.	Fight to stay alive if cornered. 1
3. Procreate.	Run away from danger. 1
	Graze. 2
	Nomadic. 2
	Eat well on good grazing. 2
	Choose a variety of grasses. 2
	Foals are naturally born at the time of spring grass growth. 2
	Seek fresh, clean water. 2
	Only one stallion per herd. 3
	Pass on dominant genes. 3
	Mares come into season in spring/summer. 3

Q10.2

HERD ANIMAL   PECKING ORDER   GRAZER   FIGHT OR FLIGHT

Q10.3

SCREAM	Anger, fear, pain if mare /gelding. If a stallion, possibly also excitement or a challenge.
NEIGH	Long-distance call to gain attention, e.g. a horse on his own in a field calling to companions.
WHINNY	High-pitched – excitement/tension, e.g. heard from mare and foal during weaning.
SQUEAL	High-pitched, short sound, e.g. mare in season.
BLOW	Frequent, quick nasal blows to draw in as much scent as possible, e.g. sniffing droppings of an unfamiliar horse.
SNORT	Short, sharp sound of fear, e.g. a young horse taken on his own into an indoor school for the first time.
NICKER	Soft, breathy sound of recognition, e.g. of a person or horse.
SIGH	Contentment, e.g. during chewing.
SNORING/GROANING	Heard during sleep.

Q10.4

INTERPRETATION	BODY LANGUAGE
HAPPY	Ears forward
INQUISITIVE	Head up, ears forward, snorting; horse may spook
PLAYFUL	Ears forward; quick movements; horse may nip/kick in play
ANXIOUS	Ears moving, head up, tense; may be unpredictable
GRUMPY	Ears back; may be aggressive
VERY GRUMPY	Ears back; threatening behaviour; seek assistance in handling

Q10.5

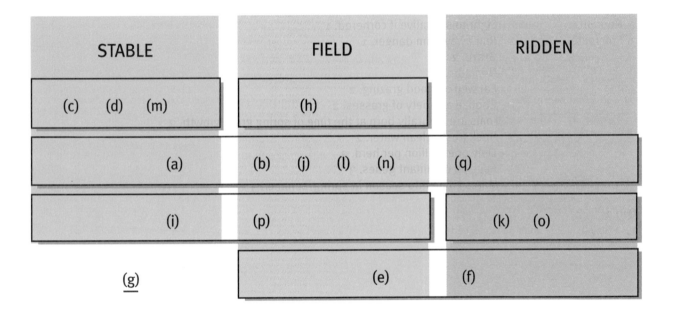

Q10.6

1. Remove other horses from the field first. HERD ANIMAL

2. Pretend to play with something in the field. CURIOSITY

3. Turn out on own and use feed bowl with food to entice. NOURISHMENT

4. Have feed ready in stable. NOURISHMENT

5. Turn out with well-fitting headcollar. OVERCOME FLIGHT INSTINCT

6. Turn out in very small grazing paddock. NOURISHMENT

7. Don't always work after catching. CREATURES OF HABIT – ASSOCIATING CATCHING WITH WORK

Q10.7

Ask a senior member of staff to demonstrate how to deal with the situation.

Q10.8

	EXPRESSION
EARS	Back, rotating
EYES	Wild, rolling, showing whites
NOSTRILS	Flared, snorting
LEGS	Will not halt, fidgets
WHOLE BODY	Tense, shakes
TAIL	Swishing

11 BASIC GRASSLAND CARE

Q11.1

FENCING	Secure. Report broken areas. Use electrical tester to check electric fencing. Fencing keeps horses securely in the field.
WATER	Fresh, constant supply available. Check automatic trough works. Water is essential for life.
GATE	Hangs properly and opens and closes well. Normally secured both sides to prevent thieves from taking the gate off its hinges. Gate is required for safe access in and out of the field.
SHELTER	In sound condition. Provides shelter from inclement weather. Possibly a thick hedge.
GRAZING	Not too sparse/too much. Food is essential for life.
GROUND	Flat, not rutted. Do not want to put unnecessary stresses on the horse's limbs.
POISONOUS PLANTS	Ragwort, deadly nightshade, foxglove, buttercup. These can be fatal if ingested.

Q11.2

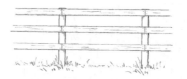

Post and rail – yes

Post and wire – yes

Electric – yes

Hedges – yes, but must be dense, high enough and free from poisonous plants

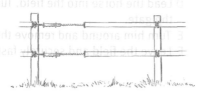

Walls – yes, but need to be high enough

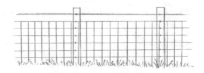

Pig netting – no

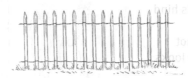

Sheep stakes – no

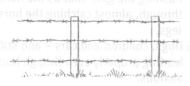

Barbed wire – no

Q11.3

Excess droppings on the ground.
Roughs (areas of sour, rank grasses because the horses produce droppings there) and lawns (areas of good, palatable grasses).
Little/no grass and many weeds.
Fencing in poor condition.
Water trough of foul water and algae.
Ground by the gate is poached.

Q11.4

Pick up droppings daily.
Implement a good seasonal grassland management plan to roll, harrow, seed, fertilise and weed-kill the fields.
Do not overstock the fields.
Clean water troughs regularly.
Maintain fencing.

Q11.5

To prevent the spread of worms and to allow palatable, good grasses to grow.

Q11.6

Horse – 1¹/₂–2 acres. Pony – 1 acre.

Q11.7

6–7 piles, well spaced out – to prevent arguments.

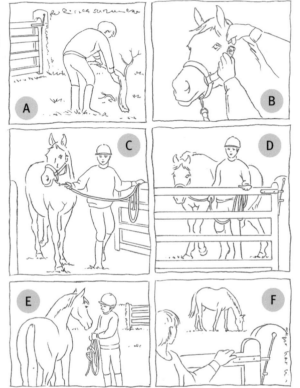

Q11.8

A Check that the route is free from hazards.
B Securely fasten the headcollar on the horse.
C Lead the horse correctly and quietly to the field.
D Lead the horse into the field. Turn him around and shut the gate.
E Turn him around and remove the headcollar.
F Leave the field and securely fasten the gate.

Q11.9

A Entering the field with a bucket of nuts.
B Leaving the gate open a little.
C Running towards the horse.
D Not fastening the headcollar properly.
E Leading in front of the horse, on the mobile phone.
F Pushing the gate shut as the horse walks through, almost catching the horse's hind legs.
G Dogs, children and cars – and still not leading properly even though horse looks anxious.

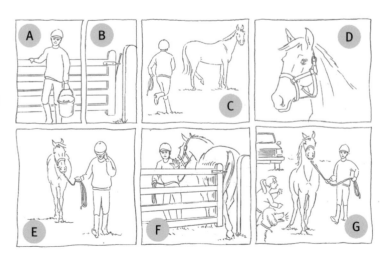

Q11.10

Take treats in pocket.
Visit and fuss all the other horses in the field first.
Leave headcollar on – leather and well fitted.
Remove the other horses from the field first.
Bring in only to feed or groom from time to time so that the horse does not always associate coming in with working.

12 WATERING AND FEEDING

Q12.1

	GOOD QUALITY HAY	BAD QUALITY HAY
SMELL	Sweet	Sour and damp
COLOUR	Golden/green	Black, dark brown
GRASSES	Quality grasses, no poisonous plants	Weeds, poisonous plants, poor grasses
DUST	No dust	Dusty
FEEL	Dry, crisp	Damp, soggy

Q12.2

ACCEPTABLE	NOT ACCEPTABLE
Does not have a strong, sweet smell	Smells sour
Brown/golden or green/golden	Dark brown or black
Inferior grasses	Weeds and poisonous plants
	Dust
Does not feel crisp and dry	Damp and soggy

Q12.3

Higher moisture content than hay.
Sweet smelling.
Separates when handled.
Golden stems.
Good grasses.

Q12.4

Respiratory problems.
Weight loss due to lack of nutrients or not eating.
Toxicity from poisonous plants, especially ragwort.
Scouring.
Sores in the corners of the mouth – occurs when grasses are hard and dry.
Colic.
Botulism – from poorly made haylage.

Q12.5

AMOUNT	Feed the correct amount according to the horse's weight, work, stabled/turned out, time of year, age, rider's ability, good doer/poor doer.
QUALITY	Feed only good quality.
HYGIENE	Cleanliness.
ROUTINE	Keep to the horse's feeding routine.
CHANGES	Make no sudden changes.
SUCCULENT	Variety and fresh vitamins.
FIBRE	Plenty of fibre.
LITTLE AND OFTEN	Feed little and often. No more than 4–5lbs (1.8–2.2kg) of feed at any time.
EXERCISE	Allow 1 hour after the horse has eaten before exercising.
WATER	Water before feeding if the horse does not have a constant supply. (This rule is now rather outdated as most horses have constant free access to water and are not led at regular intervals to a trough!)

Q12.6

- Continuous supply of fresh, clean water.
- Water before feeding.
- Keep water buckets clean and buckets deep enough for a good draught.
- Never allow the horse to drink a large amount immediately after hard exercise when he is hot.
- Do not work the horse straight after a large drink.

Q12.7

	ADVANTAGE	DISADVANTAGE
STREAM	Constant supply.	Can become poached and the horse stuck. A sand bed can give the horse sand colic. Toxic substances may accidentally contaminate the water.
BATH	Large static vessel. Can see if the horses are drinking.	Remove the taps and box in or the horse could become entangled or injured. Requires manual filling.
AUTOMATIC WATER TROUGH	Large vessel. Labour saving. Constant supply.	Cannot tell if the horses are drinking.
BUCKETS	Can see if the horses are drinking.	Labour intensive. Small, therefore need many, and strong possibility of getting knocked over.
WATER BUTTS	Can see if the horses are drinking.	Labour intensive. Preferable to buckets as they are larger and therefore less likely to be knocked over.

Q12.8

Using tie-rings on the fencing, tie the herd up and feed each individually.

If all horses in the herd have the same feed, space buckets out evenly, with one or two extra put out to prevent bullying. Remove a known bully and feed him by himself.

Q12.9

	HAY%	CONCENTRATES%
SUMMER	0 (unless poor grass)	0
AUTUMN AND SPRING	90–100 (dependent on quality of grass)	0–10 (pony nuts)
WINTER	90–100 (hay in field)	0–10 pony nuts daily

Q12.10

Hay
Haylage
Succulents
Pony cubes
Barley (possibly)
Alfalfa
Chaff
Sugar beet

Q12.11

WORKLOAD	DEFINITION	ROUGHAGE%	CONCENTRATE%
MAINTENANCE	no work	95–100	0–5
LIGHT	3–6hrs per week light hacking/schooling	80–90	10–20
MEDIUM	6–10hrs per week schooling, s-j, dressage and little competitions	70–80	20–30
HARD	10+hrs per week, hard fast and intensive work	50–70	30–50

Q12.12

16hh = 30lbs (13.6kg) of feed daily
Light work = 10–20% concentrate, 80–90% roughage
10% of 30lbs (13.6kg) = 3lbs (1.36kg)
10% concentrate = 3lbs (1.36kg)
90% roughage = 3lbs (1.36kg) x 9 = 27lbs (12.2kg)

Daily, three feeds of hay, and two concentrate feeds.

Therefore:

AM
1lb (0.45kg) pony nuts (as the horse is fizzy, it would be better not give him oats or barley as a straight)
Chaff (large handful)
8lbs (3.6kg) hay

LUNCH
8lbs (3.6kg) hay

PM
1lb (0.45kg) pony nuts
Chaff (large handful)
11lbs (4.9kg) hay (greater amount in the evening to last the night)

13 GENERAL KNOWLEDGE

Q13.1

Jodhpurs. Sturdy boots. Long sleeved top. Waterproof coat. Comfortable, well fitting trousers.

Q13.2

Bin – therefore no litter on yard.
'No smoking' signs.
Fire extinguishers.
Fire drill notice with 999 Fire Brigade number and meeting point.
Using circuit breaker.
Alarm.

Q13.3

Assess the situation.
Prevent further accidents.
Assess the casualty.
Call for help.

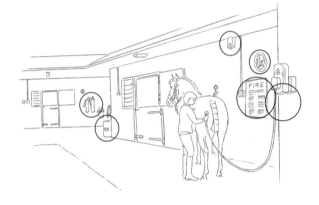

Q13.4

Airway. Breathing. Circulation.

Q13.5

A Tilt the chin back to ensure that the airway is open.
B Gently straighten the legs.
  Decide which way to roll the casualty – this may depend on surrounding obstacles.
C Kneel down and place the nearest arm up at right angles to the body.
D Bring the opposite hand to the side of the face nearest you.
E Bend the knee up furthest away from you.
F Holding the knee and keeping their hand on their face, roll the casualty over towards you. Put the thigh at right angles to the body.
G Ensure that the head is still tilted back with the airway open and that their hand is flat under their head.
H Cover them with a coat or jacket.

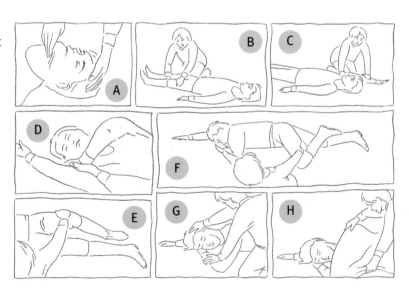

Q13.6

• If others are already in the school, ask permission to enter.
• Keep a safe distance from other horses at all times.
• Be aware of other riders at all times.
• If riding in open order, pass left hand to left hand, when at the same pace.
• Give faster paces the right of way on the outer track.
• If a rider is having problems, keep out of their way.
• If others are still riding as you leave, ask permission before exiting.

Q13.7

1 Rider and leader wearing hat, gloves and correct footwear and are carrying short whips.
2 Horse being led from the right side, with whip in right hand.
3 Half a horse's length between both horses.
4 Rider is thanking driver for slowing down.
5 The ridden horse's tack looks to be in good condition.
6 The led horse has his stirrups run up and secured to prevent them from sliding down and spooking the horse.
7 The horse is led in a bridle.
8 Horses are correctly shod.
9 Riders are wearing high visibility clothing.
10 Horses are wearing high visibility clothing.

Q13.8

Systematic training and education in all aspects of riding and horse management.
Offer guidance and help throughout with breeding and training of horses and ponies.
Actively encourage the protection of all horses and ponies.
Promote the welfare of all equines in all situations throughout the UK.

14 RIDING

Q14.1

CORRECT

1. In trot. The horse wears a running martingale. The reins remain threaded through the martingale and are therefore not taken over the head. The handler runs on the left side, by the horse's shoulder, with only the right hand holding the reins under the horse's chin. Whip in left hand.
5. Walk by shoulder, left side, reins over head, held in two hands, whip in left hand. Horse and rider looking straight ahead.

INCORRECT

2. Leading in front of the horse.
3. Walking without awareness for horse, and horse not straight or concentrating.
4. Running martingale attached, reins taken over the head to lead.
6. Dragging the horse.

Q14.2

• Shoes – secure.
• Correct tack.
• Stitching of tack is in good order.
• Girth is attached to girth straps 1 and 2 or 1 and 3.
• Numnah loops are attached to girth straps and girth.
• Latches on stirrups bars are down.
• Girth is tightened to mount.

Q14.3

Measure stirrup length along the underside of your arm.

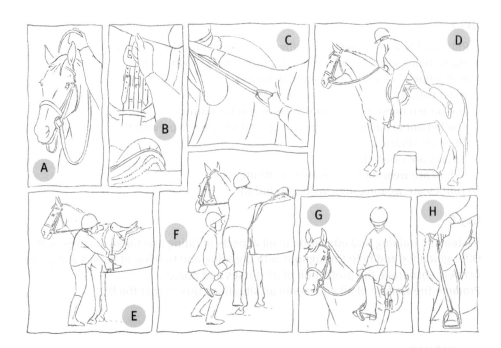

Q14.4

A Place the reins over the horse's head.

B Tighten the girth, ensuring that the numnah is pulled up into the gullet of the saddle.

C Estimate the correct length of the stirrups by positioning the leather under the arm.

either

D Mounting block. Lead the horse to the mounting block and take up the contact. Place left foot in left stirrup and lightly swing right leg over, alighting gently in the saddle.

or

E Mount from the ground. Take up the contact, face horse's tail, position left foot in left stirrup, reach for the waist of the saddle on the offside, and bounce lightly up to gently sit in the saddle.

or

F Receive a leg-up. Take up the contact, bend the left leg at the knee, discuss with the person giving the leg-up on which count to jump, jump high and lightly sit in the saddle.

G Place both feet in stirrups. In a safe area, check girth and tighten if necessary.

H Adjust stirrups as necessary, using one hand, keeping the feet in the stirrups as they are adjusted.

Q14.5

CORRECT – (A) Stirrup on the ball of the foot, turned from the front to the outside so that the leather lies flat along the lower leg.

INCORRECT – (B) Stirrup leather twisted the wrong way.

(C) Peacock safety stirrup with the elastic on the inside.

(D) Adult safety stirrup (bent iron) with the curve on the outside.

Q14.6

SIDE

Cavesson noseband fastened on the outside of the cheekpiece.

Bit too low in mouth.

Browband over ear.

Throatlash too tight.

Saddle too far back.

Stirrups too long.

Numnah slipped back under the saddle.

BEHIND

Saddle hanging to one side.

Stirrups unlevel.

Numnah not symmetrical over the horse's back.

Q14.7

Thumb on top of the reins

Little finger under the reins

Hands held about 4–6ins (10–15cm) apart, with thumbs on top

Q14.8

GOOD	BAD
Head up.	Head down.
Shoulders straight.	Shoulders rounded.
Back straight.	Back rounded.
Arms bent at the elbow.	Arms straight.
Hands held correctly.	Hands low.
Hips straight.	Hips rolled back too far.
Soft knee with a gentle bend.	Knee too far forward.
Lower leg underneath the rider.	Lower leg too far forward.
Heel directly under hip.	Heel too far forward.
Toes forward.	Toes pointing outward.

Q14.9

Having changed the rein and balanced the horse, place both reins into the outside hand. Using the inside hand, pull the whip through to the inside. Replace one rein in each hand. Position the whip correctly over the knee.

Q14.10

WALK

TROT

CANTER (left)

CANTER (right)

Q14.11

Maintain a rhythm.
Forwards enough for the rest of the ride.
Not too forwards for the rest of the ride.
Listen to instructions.
Follow instructions accurately.
Ride accurate school figures.

Q14.12

LEGS – light squeeze with the inner calf.
SEAT AND BODY – even, light weight over both seat bones. Upper body tall. Shoulders directly above hips.
HANDS – still, level contact used in a take-and-release movement.
VOICE – usually only used when lungeing or bringing on a young horse. Penalised if used in dressage competition.
WHIP – used to reinforce the leg aid with one sharp smack behind the leg. Not to be used on the shoulder.
SPURS – not used in the Stage 1 exam. Used to further refine and lighten the aid from the legs.

Q14.13

When riding on the left rein, the rider should be on the left trot diagonal. This can be recognised by looking at the horse's outside (right) shoulder, and with more experience, the rider will be able to feel whether they are right or wrong. When looking at the outside shoulder, the rider should be sitting as the shoulder moves back, and rising as it travels forwards. Being on the correct diagonal helps the horse's balance and the co-ordination of the rider's aids.

Q14.14

1 Short diagonal
2 Long diagonal
3 Centre line
4 B – E
5 Two half 20m circles, A – X, X – C
6 Two half 10m circles, E – X, X – B
7 Half 15m circle, inclining back to the track
8 Half 10m circle, inclining back to the track
9 Four-loop serpentine

FURTHER READING

The following books and booklets can all be obtained from the BHS Bookshop (address overleaf).

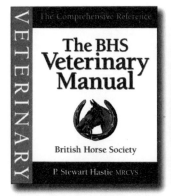

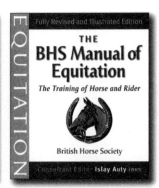
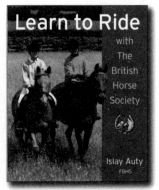

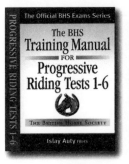

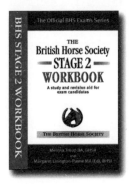
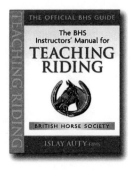

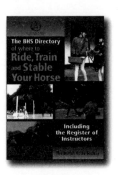

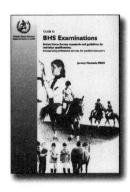

USEFUL ADDRESSES

The British Horse Society
Stoneleigh Deer Park
Kenilworth
Warwickshire
CV8 2XZ
tel: 08701 202244 or 01926 707700
fax: 01926 707800
website: www.bhs.org.uk
email: enquiry@bhs.org.uk

BHS Examinations Department
(address as above)
tel: 01926 707784
fax: 01926 707792
email:exams@bhs.org.uk

BHS Training Department
(address as above)
tel: 01926 707820
01926 707799
email: training@bhs.org.uk

BHS Riding Schools/Approvals Department
(address as above)
tel: 01926 707795
fax: 01926 707796
email: Riding.Schools@bhs.org.uk

BHS Bookshop
(address as above)
tel: 08701 201918
01926 707762
website: www.britishhorse.com